CCCC STUDIES IN WRITING & RHETORIC

Edited by Steve Parks, University of Virginia

The aim of the CCCC Studies in Writing & Rhetoric (SWR) Series is to influence how we think about language in action and especially how writing gets taught at the college level. The methods of studies vary from the critical to historical to linguistic to ethnographic, and their authors draw on work in various fields that inform composition—including rhetoric, communication, education, discourse analysis, psychology, cultural studies, and literature. Their focuses are similarly diverse—ranging from individual writers and teachers, to work on classrooms and communities and curricula, to analyses of the social, political, and material contexts of writing and its teaching.

SWR was one of the first scholarly book series to focus on the teaching of writing. It was established in 1980 by the Conference on College Composition and Communication (CCCC) in order to promote research in the emerging field of writing studies. As our field has grown, the research sponsored by SWR has continued to articulate the commitment of CCCC to supporting the work of writing teachers as reflective practitioners and intellectuals.

We are eager to identify influential work in writing and rhetoric as it emerges. We thus ask authors to send us project proposals that clearly situate their work in the field and show how they aim to redirect our ongoing conversations about writing and its teaching. Proposals should include an overview of the project, a brief annotated table of contents, and a sample chapter. They should not exceed 10,000 words.

To submit a proposal, register as an author at www.editorialmanager.com/nctebp. Once registered, follow the steps to submit a proposal (be sure to choose SWR Book Proposal from the drop-down list of article submission types).

Decolonial Possibilities

Indigenously Rooted Practices in Rhetoric and Writing

Edited by

Lisa King

University of Tennessee, Knoxville

Andrea Riley Mukavetz

City of Grand Rapids, Michigan

Conference on College Composition and Communication

NCTE National Council of Teachers of English

National Council of Teachers of English
1 E. Main St., Suite #260, Champaign, Illinois 61820
www.ncte.org

Staff Editor: Cynthia Gomez
Manuscript Editor: Bonny Graham
Series Editor: Steve Parks
Interior Design: Mary Rohrer
Cover Design: Pat Mayer
Cover Image: Ribbon skirt by Andrea Riley Mukavetz; photography by Lisa King

ISBN 978-0-8141-0239-8 (paperback); ISBN 978-0-8141-0240-4 (EPUB);
ISBN 978-0-8141-0241-1 (PDF)

Library of Congress Control Number: 2025935395

To our relatives who taught us resilience and perseverance.

To the current generation who continues the root-growing work.

To the next and future generations, may we do right by you.

CONTENTS

FOREWORD: MENDING THE TEARS

THIS IS A STORY.

I have been living a different life these days, mostly outside of academia. In this life, I practice giving thanks before moving forward with teaching. Since it feels odd, false, performative to do so here in print, I would appreciate it if you, dear reader, would take a moment to send your gratitude out in the four directions (east, south, west, and north) as well as to the sky above, the earth below, and the waters all around. That way, we can all move forward in the same state of mind.

Now that we are together, I will begin this story by acknowledging that I am writing on the seized and occupied homelands of the Red Willow peoples of Taos Pueblo. Specifically, I sit on a piece of land that was part of the Lucero de Godoi land grant from the Spanish colonial government—a parcel that was taken back by the Taos peoples during Popé's Rebellion in 1680 but regained by the Spanish in 1696 when it became part of the Antonio Martinez land grant that effectively installed Spanish colonial settlement and control of these Tiwa homelands. I offer thanks and respect to contemporary Tiwa peoples and to their ancestors for their persistence and patience in continuing to maintain right relations in this place despite the impacts of colonization.

The story I'm telling here isn't long, but it is braided through stories from a number of elders, ancestors, descendants, and myself. By now it's commonplace to hear me speak of story. I am, like MariJo Moore, "a storied woman" (Powell 11). In fact, I believe that we *all* are storied in complex theoretical and material ways, that our lives are interconnected and storied alongside the lives of all living and spirit beings. These days even scientists agree that trees are alive and that they communicate, that crows and ravens have consciousness and that they remember and share stories, that the mycelium network is vibrantly alive and communicative. I could go on, but I won't. It's good that scientists have started to believe what Indigenous peoples have known all along. It's good that more human beings are waking up to the truth of how we are only one kind of living, thinking, storied being here on the earth. Still, carrying stories in the way that I (and so many others) have carried them over the past decades has not been an easy thing.

I carry story. I live story. I breathe and eat and dream story. Story comes to me through ancestors, spirits, and the land. Story comes in the morning as the sun rises over Pueblo Peak here in the Sangre de Cristo Mountains of the southern Rockies. Story comes at night as the stars do their dance and the twinkling mist of the Milky Way spreads itself across the sky. Story comes creeping alongside when I walk in the forest, foraging and harvesting and speaking with the trees. Story wraps itself around me in ceremony. Story—in spirit and in fact—is always with me, and with you. I am made of story . . . and so are you. Story is a theoretical, methodological, material, and spiritual presence that holds the web of life, of our relations, together. Story holds the universe together. But having spent more than three decades trying to persuade academics of the centrality of story, I can honestly say that I am tired, and I am grateful that the scholars, teachers, writers, and editors in this collection have taken up the task of listening to, speaking, and carrying story. And that they've learned to hold those stories from spirits, from ancestors, from the land, from our lives in such a way that they've found new energy to keep telling them to academic audiences who are beginning to learn to hear.

A specific story. A long time ago, I wrote an essay in which I called out a famous American Indian literature scholar for claiming that Indigenous people did not theorize. As I workshopped drafts of that essay, I started noticing some common responses about how it was much too early in my career to start critiquing the "big" scholars. This response was as common from fellow BIPOC grad students as it was from trusted professors and mentors. And it's a response that began to make me deeply uncomfortable, angry even. Every single person who read a draft of this essay agreed that it was dead-on accurate, but they all also agreed that I should pull the punches. The thing is, I didn't come to academia to pull those "hey, I noticed you're acting like a colonizer" punches. I came to help make Native knowledge-making, Native scholarship, and Native peoples more visible and valued—a set of tasks that required *noticing* and *calling out* colonialism and how it continues to be enacted, replicated, and sustained in academia. I remember thinking that I'd already slogged through a lot of academic hazing and tradition-keeping, and if I couldn't do this academic gig the way I wanted to do it, well, it just didn't seem worth doing. So I didn't soften the critique; in fact, I sharpened it.

When that piece, "Blood and Scholarship: One Mixed-Blood's Story," came out in Keith Gilyard's important *Race, Rhetoric, and Composition* in 1999, I was suddenly surrounded by a mass of other graduate students saying "thank you" for that sharpness. It's still a piece that BIPOC scholars connect with for precisely that reason—suddenly, someone with a lot to lose was (as they say in the parlance today) saying the quiet part out loud. Twenty-five years later, and I've never regretted my decision to do that. In fact, I've encouraged, mentored, and supported scores of new scholars as they learned to do the same—be genuine and humble and absolutely say the quiet parts out loud. I'd like to think that a small part of this collection is a result of those decades of work.

In many ways, over the past decades I've watched many of my colleagues in rhetoric and writing studies come, not just to understand the blood that I was seeing, but to see it themselves. The "progress" so desired by liberals and, not coincidentally, by settler colonialism itself, then, is being made. As I worked and lived in academia, however, I began to understand its deep and utter complicity in the colonial project, the degree to which those bloody walls were a fetish for the liberal progressives who actually hold the coloniality of the university together. But I understand it now. The essays in this collection are an attempt by scholars more optimistic than I to shake the certainty of liberal progressivism, to create space for Indigenous knowledges inside the belly of the beast itself, and to create acceptance and support for the Indigenous peoples who have made their home inside that beast (if only for the handful of years it takes to get a degree).

What I feel still needs to be said, not as a critique of this beautiful collection of work but as an alongside to it, is this: I struggled mightily for years to persuade my perfectly nice colleagues (many who saw themselves as allies to Indigenous and BIPOC peoples) that these colonial systems actually existed and were damaging in both their intent and their effect. I was shamed, beloved, queried, and stonewalled in those persuasions. I mean, how could such genocidal oppression survive in the face of very good people with very good intentions trying hard to make sure the BIPOC and LGBTQ+ folks were taken seriously and given equal opportunity? How indeed. My life in community for the past few years has not only taught me "how" but also shown me the degree to which academics are desperately, implacably naïve about their own complicity in colonialism and the many forms (racism, capitalism, sexism, homophobia, etc.) it still takes in our daily lives. Believe me, Indigenous peoples in the community understand completely that the academy is a colonial institution, one that eats the souls of people who try to change it. Even further, that understanding isn't limited to Indigenous peoples, or to BIPOC folks. Folks who actually live their lives in alliance with the earth itself understand where colonialism resides, where it feeds, where it proliferates—in the ideological state apparatuses of our not-quite-not-fascist social, state, and federal institutions, and in the human cultures that take the boundaries of those institutions as truth. And, yes, this includes the so-called liberal university. But I digress.

In the face of these colonial academic truths, the work displayed in this collection takes enormous courage and energy and dedication to the students and communities they serve and the systems they endure. It reminds me a bit of a poem I kept tucked inside my journal all throughout graduate school and well into my life as a professor, a poem that I'd read to remind myself of what I was supposed to be doing in order to stay on the path of story and to avoid, as much as academia would let me, a path of ego and self-centeredness: Paula Gunn Allen's "Grandmother." In this poem, Allen tells the story of Grandmother Spider, who wove "the strands / of her body, her pain, her vision / into creation" and then disappeared and left the work of weaving "blankets into tales of life, / memories of light and ladders, / infinity-eyes, and rain" to human beings. As the poem ends, Allen tells us that now she herself sits on a "laddered rain-bearing rug /and mend[s] the tear with string" (264–65). That last line still reverberates with the beauty and the difficulty of Indigenous and decolonial work inside the academy—we have only string to mend this glorious, silver, silken rug that is the reality of all creation, but we *must* use what we have in order to hold the web together. Even today I read that line and think, "Did I do enough?" But then I think of all the beautiful, kind, smart, fierce, determined humans I've been privileged to know through academia, how they are loose in the world and the discipline and are continuing to mend the tears of colonization, to delink from its violences as much as they can, and to carry the stories of that work forward into the future.

I know it has become fashionable these days for scholars to claim decolonial methodology or theory as simply another way to make themselves look better, hipper, more woke. They use the language of that theory or methodology as a weapon in the usual academic way of bullying and narcissism and a certainty in the claim that they *know* what it means to engage in this work while others don't. One thing I know for sure is that almost *none of us* knows precisely how to do decolonizing work in a way that doesn't get all tangled up in colonial institutions—and the few holy people who do have the most complete knowledge of how to do that work certainly aren't living in academia, or even talking to it much. What I *have* learned from medicine people is that work isn't about *you* or *me*; it's about the survival and health of the community. It isn't so much about what understanding or set of practices *you* or *I* have come to possess; it's about how those understandings and practices support the web of relations, beginning with communities of folks who've been at the pointy end of colonization for hundreds of years. Learning to delink from colonizing practices is not (and cannot be) a personal badge of honor, nor an end point; it is, instead, the sheer beginning of learning to be a better relative, just a start at taking responsibility for the ways we *all* benefit from colonialism, the literal wake-up call for creating *something else* together. Delinking is, in fact, the bare minimum acknowledgment of the reciprocity we owe to all of our nonhuman relations.

One of the things I like about the pieces in this collection is that each writer, teacher, scholar, mentor is deeply involved both in taking responsibility and in supporting a more balanced and healthy web of relations, both inside and outside the academy. In these pages, we have Tekobbe, Wieser-Weryackwe, Brownlee, Jennings, and Shade-Johnson focusing on students (graduate and undergraduate) as real human communities who deserve to be treated as valued relatives through expanded pedagogical and relational engagements. Then there's King, Evans Garriott, and Whitebear, who are trying to build real human communities of responsibility and reciprocity among their immediate colleagues and across their institutions, while Cedillo brings that same community-building focus into our broader understanding of scholarly relations and our typical (aka colonial) practices. Finally, we have Riley Mukavetz and Bardwell doing the hard work of connecting and weaving local Tribal knowledge and practices into a reciprocity-centered conversation with academic and institutional systems. From my perspective, this gathering of humans is doing the hard work as they acknowledge, listen, honor, and act in order to figure out how reciprocity and responsibility can actually work in this imperfect world. We need more of this in every facet of our lives, but especially here in academia where we tend to build insular intellectual walls that separate us from the lives of everyone else—everything else—on the planet.

Notice, dear readers, how each of these folks is less concerned with claiming/homesteading academic territory and much more focused on making the experience of learning, teaching, and scholarship more welcoming, supportive, and simply livable for other human beings. No one is saying something here for the sheer sake of saying it; every single contributor is concerned with the "why" and "how" and "so what" consequences of their work. For me, this is what it means to begin to decolonize and delink, to say the quiet parts out loud, and to begin to engage with our academic lives here in the belly of the beast. These contributors—these beautifully imperfect humans—show us what it looks like to shift our attention away from those traditional scholarly behaviors that are mired in competition, exceptionalism, and destruction. They turn instead toward the well-being of fellow humans, acting with a good heart, and keeping a laser focus on building—spaces, ideas, structures—community in which relationships are real commitments that require responsibility, reciprocity, love, and care. This, my friends, is the work I dreamed about all those years ago, work that acknowledges academia as both a system built on blood and bones and one that involves a kind of participation that allows us to be humans, grateful servants of the earth and the web of relations. Humans. Made from stardust, our reality woven from the body of Grandmother Spider, our lives inextricably connected to one another and the well-being of this beautiful planet where we all must live.

WORKS CITED

Allen, Paula Gunn. "Grandmother." *New Worlds of Literature: Writing from America's Many Cultures,* edited by Jerome Beaty and J. Paul Hunter, Norton, 1989, pp. 264–65.

Powell, Malea. "Blood and Scholarship: One Mixed-Blood's Story." *Race, Rhetoric, and Composition*, edited by Keith Gilyard, Boynton/Cook, 1999, pp. 1–16.

Malea Powell
Michigan State University

ACKNOWLEDGMENTS

Lisa: Anyone who's worked on a project like this knows that it takes a whole community to make it happen. I want to offer deepest thanks and gratitude to my coeditor, sister, and friend, Andrea Riley Mukavetz, as we've kept this project alive through a pandemic, illness, major career shifts, raising our kids, and life in general. Huge thanks are owed to our contributors to this collection, who have hung with us through the process and shared their stories and experiences in such thoughtful and wonderful ways, and to the NCTE/CCCC American Indian Caucus for being such a supportive community. Many thanks to Steve Parks, former editor of the Studies in Writing & Rhetoric (SWR) series, who first suggested we do a project like this and invited us to challenge the discipline and institutions we both invest ourselves in so deeply and also struggle with. I'm also incredibly grateful to the students, colleagues, and friends at the University of Tennessee, Knoxville, who have been doing the hard work to support Native and Indigenous voices and change at our institution, particularly Ellen Lofaro, Brooke Bauer, Joy Harjo, Julie Reed, Cat Shteynberg, Sadie Counts, Claudio Gómez, Emily Reichard, Kim Smith, Nat Welch, Carrie Sheffield, Stella Takvoryan, Pilar Garcia, Peter Cates, Maggie Diedrich, Joshua Ortiz Baco, Danny Dominguez, Allie Hicks, Sara Ritchey, Micah Swimmer, Dani Rimbach-Jones, Jud Laughter, Amber Kent-Johnson, Kelly Sauskojus, Amy Elias, Jessie Tanner, MaryLeauna Christensen, and Michelle Brown. Finally, as always, I am so grateful to my husband and my son, without whom I wouldn't have the wherewithal to keep going—Thorsten and Julian, you keep me fed, you keep me rooted, and you remind me what matters outside of the job and the institution.

Andrea: This edited collection was an experience in patience, understanding, collaboration, grief, and joy. I still can't believe that it has finally come to fruition. The pandemic took so much from us, especially in Tribal Nations communities, including multiple incredible contributors who had to withdraw. Toward the end of the process, I chose a career shift outside of academia and into community engagement and local government. This was a decision based on a calling and a need for a new challenge, but my investment in expanding the knowledge and approaches of Indigenous rhetorics continues. I am grateful to the contributors, reviewers, and editors of the SWR series who have ensured that this project continued and became published. I am especially grateful to my older sister and collaborator, Lisa King, for her mentorship, friendship, and solidarity. We spent so much time bringing this book to the finish line, and in the process we bore witness to our children growing, our own wrinkles developing, and tenure and promotion, and a shared love for romance novels and gardens developed as well. Last, dear reader, thank you for reading, teaching, or citing this book. We all know that the power of citation and knowledge sharing contributes to the root-growing work we strive for here.

INTRODUCING OURSELVES

Lisa King and Andrea Riley Mukavetz

> The value of resistance is the reclaiming of the sacred and significant self.
>
> —Lee Maracle, *Memory Serves*

> Treating decolonial as a metonym for social justice or critical-cultural action colonizes decolonization.
>
> —Cana Uluak Itchuaqiyaq and Breeanne Matheson, "Decolonial Dinners"

BEFORE WE BEGIN, LET US introduce ourselves and our relationship to each other. That's a good place to start so that you get a sense of where we're coming from.

Aanii Lisa—nimisenh,

My older sister, I'm writing this to you while we are all enduring a pandemic. In so many ways, the pandemic has made me understand how unimportant and important this collection is. Unimportant, as we have delayed or moved at the slowest, bravest turtle pace to ensure that our relatives, the contributors of this collection, could be here while we are navigating the death, illness, and long-term impacts of this pandemic. And also important, because I think we both know what our Indigenous relatives, inside and outside of academia, are enduring, as well as the resistances that are being mobilized. I know how much Indigenous students, faculty, and staff need people to join our efforts in making Indigenous space in our institutions and within rhetoric and composition to imagine Indigenous futures.

Nimisenh, I keep referring to you as "my older sister" because this is how I understand our relationship to each other and our roles in rhetoric and composition. Together we are co-chairs of the American Indian Caucus of NCTE/CCCC. And also you have done so much for me personally to support my scholarship and research agenda. Many times I have wanted to give up or have thought my scholarship doesn't matter, and you have always been there to cheer me on and show me its impact. This is what it looks like to love and mentor in our caucus through Indigenous worldviews: we take seriously the beliefs around relations and relatives because the survival of present and future generations is tantamount to decoloniality, to cultural continuance, to imagining new possibilities. Miigwetch, nimisenh.

This collection came out of recognizing, as always, a gap in our disciplinary conversations around the relationship between decolonial theory and practice and Indigenous rhetorics. It came out of, as always, noticing that our scholarship, worldviews, and pedagogical practices were being presented on, discussed, and published without fully engaging in the complex understanding of settler colonialism, Indigeneity, and rhetoric on Turtle Island.[1]

Lisa, I am thinking about all the important work your collection, *Survivance, Sovereignty, and Story*, did to make visible the relationship between Indigenous rhetorics and Indigenous pedagogical practice. For me, this collection is a continuation of that work—it seeks to engage with the frameworks and beliefs of decolonial theory and practice, address how decoloniality and Indigeneity are always intertwined, and make space for contributors to authentically grapple with the hard work—the seriously hard work—of being in academia and making Indigenous, decolonial space in our classrooms, research, publications, and professional work.

Andrea

Koolamalsi,[2] Andrea,

I think the first time we really shared space together was at a casual gathering at the conference hotel at the 2012 St. Louis Conference on College Composition and Communication (CCCC) Convention. I had heard about you and you had been introduced to me as an up-and-coming scholar, but I hadn't had a chance to get to know you yet. Many of the folks from the American Indian Caucus were there, and I have a vivid memory of watching you watching those of us outside your cohort, wary and curious. I remembered what it was like to start trying to network while moving toward the job market while wondering if work in cultural rhetorics and especially Indigenous rhetorics would ever be valued—hell, I had been trying to fight for a place for four years at that point, postgraduation—and I wanted so much to reassure you that we had your back. I'm so glad we are working on this project now, together. Those of us invested in cultural rhetorics, Indigenous rhetorics, and decolonial work have all been slowly, haltingly, determinedly, and exhaustedly building relationships, reimagining what academia could be, and trying to make community in those awkward conference settings where competition, not care, sets too much of the tone too much of the time.

Since then I've gotten to cradle your sweet babies, sit at tables across the country and laugh or cry or vent or tell stories, and I'm so glad to know you. It's the community we build with our relations that makes all of this worth it in an academic climate that never imagined us doing work like this to start with. Your fire, your hope, and your example push me to do better, to keep going.

This project is grown from the roots put down by senior mentors and scholars, spreading like a patch of sweetgrass that sprouts above ground with its prolific long, slim leaves but is just as powerful, if not more so, as it extends its life and reach through its roots. Rhizomes like this can be cut off or damaged or harvested from the top, but they grow back. That's how I imagine this work: knowing the energy is underground, watching new growth emerge over time, and knowing that even if that growth isn't immediately welcomed above, there's a network of roots to support trying again.

Andrea, I know you and I both have our stories about how this goes. Academia, and rhetoric and composition as a field, are not places that were ever meant to support the growth of decolonial work. The university/college/educational setting as we know it is of a settler-colonial design meant to embody in its students a particular way of interacting with the world that has frequently set humans (of European descent) apart from and in domination over everything and everyone else. For all the diversity in branches of study, there's a unifying fiction that the ways of understanding the world that derive from Euro-Western concepts and keeping ourselves outside of that process of understanding, detached, is somehow best. That's not to say that all the things we learn and do in academic spaces are useless. It's the uncritical taking for granted that it's the best way, the right way, and the only way, when it was transplanted and cultivated deliberately overtop Indigenous ways of knowing, being, and doing, that's such a huge problem.

We are now or have been employed by this system.

We've worked for tenure or some kind of security in this system.

It would bind us, grow over us, choke us, and consume us alive if we let it.

Kudzu academia.

But we—and here I mean the network of teachers, scholars, administrators, and mentors doing the same kind of work that we're doing—are searching for ways to make possible different conceptions of what education or rhetoric or writing or communicating might be. Tapping into decolonial ways of thinking and doing, this collection centers practices and discussions rooted in Indigenous North America as a way to imagine and enact decolonial possibilities.

This is our hope, and what follows is our offering to you, dear reader, as a way to help you think through these possibilities in your context, on the land you live on, within your relationships on Turtle Island.

Lisa

NOTE

1. Turtle Island is a frequently used Indigenous way to refer to what is now known as North America. There are many tribally specific stories that tell the creation of the land as being shaped on a turtle's back, which is why the land looks like a turtle. We choose to use this label to describe the

land base to honor those stories and the names of this land before settler colonialism.

2. I am a beginning learner of the Munsee language and am indebted to Ian McCallum and the late Karen Mosko (both of the Munsee-Delaware Nation) for the opportunity to begin learning and to support this beautiful language. I use it here with permission, even so briefly, to help make it visible.

Introduction: Interventions to Highlight Decolonial Possibilities and Connections in Rhetoric and Writing Studies

Lisa King and Andrea Riley Mukavetz

WHEN WE DECIDED ON THE TITLE of the collection, we chose *possibilities* because we believe by beginning with Indigeneity and colonization, our discipline can have more complex, nuanced, intentional, and thorough relationships with the ideas of "rhetoric" and "rhetorical practice." We therefore offer you the perspectives in this book as another site of decolonial emergence; as we'll discuss, other scholars have done significant root-growing work, and we intend this to be new and medicinal growth—not invasive, dominating growth—in the direction of decolonial practice. What we offer here is a range of viewpoints from both Indigenous scholars and relatives who have taken up the call to decolonize the university in whatever way it can be, from publishing to administrative work to teaching. The chapters here come from active members of the American Indian Caucus (AIC) at the Conference on College Composition and Communication (CCCC) and its allies, an organization that has always been a network of Indigenous scholars and allies.[1]

Decolonial work must stretch into every facet of our discipline, must be cultivated, must be nurtured. We fully recognize the inertia of higher education and its reliance on taking its existence as "good" for granted. What we hope this collection of essays can do is provide ways to rethink our everyday practices in the field with the goal of making decolonial possibilities a reality. We don't intend for this collection to be taken up as a "how to" checklist to decolonize the classroom. Instead, this introduction and the collection of stories that follow are meant to serve as a theoretical and disciplinary intervention into how the discipline of rhetoric and composition understands, practices, and theorizes decoloniality and decolonization in our research, teaching, and professional relationships.

REORIENTING TO THEORIZING WITH THIS LAND, TURTLE ISLAND

We come to you as scholars of and in the subfield of Indigenous rhetorics. As Andrea mentioned in her opening letter, this collection builds on the edited collection *Survivance, Sovereignty, and Story* (L. King, R. Gubele, and J. R. Anderson), which displays a broad view of Indigenous rhetorics pedagogical practice. This collection addresses an Indigenous rhetorics paradigm for theorizing and enacting decoloniality. As Kimberly Wieser-Weryackwe and colleagues note in the introduction to the recently published annotated bibliography on American Indian and Indigenous rhetorics, there is a relationship between Indigenous rhetorics and cultural rhetorics due to the shared value and methodology of relationality. There is also a relationship between American Indian studies and Indigenous rhetorics. For Indigenous rhetoricians, our rhetorical tradition draws from Indigenous studies, which includes literary criticism and carries these theories and paradigms into rhetoric and writing to examine *how* Indigenous intellectuals engage in knowledge making through a triad of body, space, and culture (Davis). As Andrea Riley Mukavetz notes,

> Native rhetorics positions its scholarship and teaching within decolonial theories and social movements because of its commitment to privileging Indigenous ways of knowing, acknowledging one's complicity in colonial rhetorics, and developing options for creating and sharing knowledge that does not use colonial rhetorical practices. (109)

In "Iñupiat Ilitqusiat: An Indigenist Ethics Approach for Working with Marginalized Knowledges in Technical Communication,"

Itchuaqiyaq notes that an Indigenous research paradigm and decolonial practice are interconnected. The mode she provides "center[s] ancestral knowledge and Tribal responsibility in ways that ask individuals to understand who they are, how they represent themselves and the world around them, and how they affect others" (37). Native rhetorics, then, serve as both intervention and another option for understanding the relationship between settler colonialism, imperialism, and language. As Angela Haas writes, "I challenge myself, the discipline, my colleagues, and my students to consider how the language we use might serve to redress the long-standing legacies of colonialism and imperialism, particularly in the rhetoric that we choose to employ to represent our work and the work of others" (288). We take on Haas's challenge as one of the goals of this collection and offer it as an invitation for collective work toward the future.

We absolutely recognize that we are not the first scholars to take up the question of decolonial or decolonizing work in rhetoric and composition. For example, recent book publications include Iris Ruiz and Raúl Sánchez's *Decolonizing Rhetoric and Composition Studies: New Latinx Keywords for Theory and Pedagogy*; Romeo García and Damián Baca's edited collection, *Rhetorics Elsewhere and Otherwise: Contested Modernities, Decolonial Visions*; Jennifer Clary-Lemon and David Grant's edited collection, *Decolonial Conversations in Posthuman and New Material Rhetorics*; and Romeo García and colleagues' edited collection, *Pluriversal Literacies: Tools for Perseverance and Livable Futures.* In their own ways, these texts have presented various approaches to working with decoloniality and decolonization as concepts for consideration in rhetoric and composition, and the contributors to these volumes have valuable insights to offer.

Yet while this most recent work has at least gestured toward Indigenous peoples of Turtle Island or begun the work of trying to thread Indigenous conversations into the fabric of ongoing scholarly conversations, we still assert that something is out of balance in the larger pattern. Overall, Indigenous rhetorics are still considered to be marginal, even though they are ever present in our field and on this land (specifically, for our focus here, North America).

We need more consistent grounding in and engagement with the decolonizing work on this land. In general, we are concerned with both the intentional and the unintentional omissions of the existence of Tribal Nations people—including the actual knowledge and lived experiences and the scholarship of Indigenous rhetoricians who have been publishing at the intersections of decolonial theory and rhetoric and composition. We are open and willing to engage with many models and approaches to decolonial theory. But we are concerned: to omit, ignore, or erase Indigenous contributions and presence from decolonial theory on Turtle Island *while writing, teaching, and living on Turtle Island* is an active engagement of settler colonialism and conquest of ideas. It is, as Malea Powell writes in "Blood and Scholarship," how "homesteading as a scholarly practice becomes an expectation for academics." These rules are what Powell calls a "second-wave genocide." She writes, "Not only does the imperial power commit material acts meant to crush an unruly Indigenous population but also its institutions of intellectual and cultural exchange (i.e., universities) make the rules by which the first-wave genocide will be studied, and these same rules apply to the study of genocide survivors" (4). In this scenario, to omit the contributions and survivance of Tribal Nations people from theorizing and defining decolonization is to commit the next stage of genocide: it is to fulfill the act that settlers were unable to do—wipe our existence away. Itchuaqiyaq provides a Tribally centered approach to enacting decoloniality in research. Similar to arguments she and Matheson made in "Decolonizing Decoloniality," she writes, "For those who wish to follow decolonial methods in their work, a shift in one's research paradigm as well as one's own personal paradigm is almost universally necessary in order to enact decoloniality instead of merely using 'decolonize' as a catch-all term appropriate to mean human rights or social justice" (Iñupiat 37).

This project, like all others dealing with decolonial and decolonizing theory and praxis, is a work in progress. It's a snapshot in time and place that reflects the exigences, questions, and needs that we and our contributors are facing, and it is the culmination-for-now—though not the stopping point—of many of our conversations about how to live and be and do in the field and subfields of rhetoric and composition. Our goal is to engage with Lisa Brooks's understanding of mapping as a participatory, local, Indigenous knowledge-making practice and to map the possibilities of decolonial theory and decoloniality. As cultural rhetoricians, we seek to help constellate those possibilities for rhet comp. While we take a kinship-based approach to mapping decolonial possibilities in this introduction and offer our own connections to these scholars, activists, and territories, we need to make something clear: There is no "decolonial" without addressing Indigeneity. There is no decolonial theory without the consistent, active, and engaged citation of Indigenous scholars of Turtle Island. There is no practice of decoloniality without addressing—actively, even for those scholars who identify as historically oppressed, "of color"—the truth that you do so on Indigenous land.

Susan Sleeper-Smith et al. have already emphatically made the argument that there is no American history without Indigenous history. J Kēhaulani Kauanui's work has clearly articulated that just as white studies can't be a thing by itself and must exist in relationship to all the other racial constructs that make up "whiteness," settler colonial studies can't be a thing without careful engagement with Indigenous studies and Indigenous peoples. Craig Womack has asserted that Native American literatures are the central trunk of the literary tree and not grafted-on branches to a European canon. And both Lyons and Powell ("Rhetorics," "Down") have argued that any "rhetorical tradition" in the Americas should be centering Indigenous rhetorical practices, not treating them as exotic ancillaries to the "real" rhetorical tradition. Effective decolonizing work must always be threaded through with the attendant acknowledgment and obligations to the land and the Indigenous peoples who are connected to it. Likewise, for our purposes here, we do not see how decolonizing work in rhetoric and composition can be separated from Indigenous studies and Indigenous worldviews. The root of rhetorical and composition practices on these lands always connect back to Indigenous peoples. To ignore Indigenous rhetorics is an act of settler colonialism.

In this collection, we operate through the understanding that decoloniality existed first, in nonacademic Indigenous communities, as survivance—as cultural continuance—as a response to colonialism and white supremacy. Like most Indigenous knowledges, it is obvious to us because it reflects our ongoing efforts of survivance and cultural continuance. We, descended as we are, are proof that our ancestors' decolonial efforts worked or we would not be here. This understanding is, in many ways, a complicated effort because to communicate our existence and brilliance is to translate and explain how our knowledges are both ancient and new. As Lee Maracle once remarked on decoloniality, you can preserve peaches but you'd have a tough time getting a dance or song into a mason jar (cited in Brooks). For us, this means that decoloniality, like Indigenous cultures, is alive. It is active and ongoing and will continue to change and develop as older generations are informed by younger generations; as land claims continue to be fought, lost, and won; and as we fight for our water and our bodies.

This edited collection, like a tobacco pouch, is an offering. It is a gift provided to both settlers and Indigenous people, of those whose ancestors were stolen and kidnapped and those who continue to understand what it means to live on Turtle Island with an ongoing legacy of settler colonialism and white supremacy. It's intended to shape the next generation of contributions of what constitutes Indigenous rhetorics and to invite all of us to consider what it means to do rhetorical studies and to teach on stolen, settled, Indigenous land.

In the following sections, we offer an overview of the concepts that drive decolonial and decolonizing work for us and then provide a précis of the chapters our contributors have woven for us. This is indeed a story, our story, as we know that every person makes their theory journey from their own place and positionality. Rather than providing set definitions of *decolonial* and *decolonizing*, each contributor (including us) instead offers what these terms mean to them in the work they do. We do not claim the final word, but we do claim that our story here is another entry point for decolonial possibilities that the contributors take up and illustrate. We've already introduced ourselves/each other; now we want to reflect on the thinkers who have brought us to this place and time, and then offer our goals for this collection as an invitation to you, dear reader, to contemplate your journey and begin formulating a plan of action for your place and your moment. Miigwetch, anushiik, thank you for reading.

WHAT DECOLONIALITY AND DECOLONIZATION MEAN TO US: OUR RELATIONS OUTSIDE OF TURTLE ISLAND

As part of our work as editors, we've been asked to define *decoloniality* and *decolonization*. Within the typical academic framework, we're supposed to take on the mantle of authoritative knowledge and set parameters for what constitutes acceptable ideas. That is colonial logics at work, in the sense that a colonizing institution sets the boundaries on what kinds of knowledge are "good" or "acceptable." For our purposes here, we're not interested in saying which definition is right or best, but rather where the definition, approach, or paradigm leads, how and why it is useful, and how it aids us in getting the work done. We've also tried to make space for the contradictions, the pain, the ideas left unfigured-out, to honor the belief that like identity, like Indigenous futures, there is still so much to be decided. Yet we have identified some commonalities among the theories, practices, and trajectories of decoloniality and decolonial theory, such as being grounded in place, people, and context, and in the investment in sovereignty, self-determination, or cultural continuance. And there are moments of contradictions and deviations, specifically the roles of decolonial theory and settlers. That said, we want to share some of the powerful work from a variety of Indigenous academic elders and allies who can help shape the ways we approach defining decoloniality. Each of us comes from a different set of experiences, and so each of us offers our observations here.

Andrea

Often I am asked, "What is the difference between decoloniality, decolonization, and decolonial theory?" To answer this, we need to begin in the space where postcolonial theory and decolonial theory lived together and where "post-co" pushed itself to become decolonial. Specifically, I am thinking about Black intellectuals such as Fanon, Césaire, Dei, and Thiong'o. Indigenous to land bases such as Martinique, Ghana, and Kenya, these authors wrote about the complexity of living within settled, occupied land while encouraging resistance, rebellion, and, at times, violence to delink from the colonial rhetorical practices that argued their Indigenous literacies and worldviews were subordinate and not worthy to be included in academia. Their arguments continue to have weight as the impact of colonialism on knowledge has become increasingly visible. For example, each scholar emphasized the importance of delinking from ideological colonial knowledge-making practices and reorienting to territory-specific Indigenous knowledges, reclaiming and celebrating the writing and speaking of Indigenous languages, and incorporating regionally Indigenous literature into curriculum and pedagogy (Dei), as well as acknowledging how we are all complicit in colonial impact even while trying to break free of colonial occupation (Fanon; Césaire). These scholars from different land bases were grappling with whether they truly were postcolonial if their land bases, cultural practices, and institutions of thought and teaching invested in the beliefs, histories, and frameworks of those who colonized them. Fanon's arguments on the role of violence and decolonization are crucial to this discussion—must one enact actual violence to free oneself from the colonial state or from the epistemic and generational violence that was and is endured? To engage in decolonial practice, then, requires deconstruction and reconstruction. It must employ Indigenous knowledges to both break apart a structure and imagine new possibilities. Tiffany Lethabo King theorizes this relationship between Black diaspora studies and Indigenous studies as a space between postcolonial and decolonial theory, an important space of alliance and new–ancient critical frameworks. For her, the metaphor and actual space of the Black Shoal "functions as critique of normative discourses within colonial, settler colonial, and postcolonial studies that narrowly posit land and labor as the primary frames from which to theorize colonial, anti-Indigenism, and anti-Black racism" (11).

These scholars provide important interventions into academia and its investment in canons and frameworks that define the rhetorical traditions as literary and intellectual, as well as offer real strategies for how to pay attention to the relationship between colonial impact and knowledge production. Walter Mignolo's *The Darker Side of Western Modernity* was a field-changing book. His framework of understanding colonialism as a matrix of power acutely named what global Indigenous people have been saying for a long time. And this is also important to address: Mignolo is careful in his citational practices and framing to acknowledge that his theories are not new. He continues the work of decolonial theory by parsing through both decoloniality and decolonization. Decoloniality constitutes the ideological components of decolonialism; it addresses how to delink epistemologically from the colonial matrix of power. Decolonization is a movement, a series of resistances and rebellions to take control of the state. Mignolo traces this to Africa and Asia during the Cold War, a move I am grateful for because it addresses Indigeneity and colonialism on a global level.

Lisa

My own journey in learning about decolonial practices from academic elders I can trace to Linda Tuhiwai Smith and Haunani-Kay Trask. Smith is now, I believe, the most-cited Indigenous scholar in the world, and that's no accident: her academia-altering book, *Decolonizing Methodologies: Research and Indigenous Peoples*, now in its third edition, clearly articulates why "research" carried and still carries deeply negative connotations for Indigenous peoples around the globe. When academic institutions extract, manipulate, and appropriate knowledge from Indigenous peoples, those institutions are embodying and enacting colonial structures to the detriment of Indigenous peoples. Only if and when research and teaching are done with the purpose of deconstructing colonialism and for the benefit and support of Indigenous peoples *on Indigenous peoples' terms* are we going to begin seeing opportunities to make education and knowledge-making in academia more than a reinforcement of colonial ideologies and epistemologies. This was formative for me as a graduate student and remains key. In her introduction to the third edition, Smith argues that even though much has been accomplished since *Decolonizing Methodologies* was first published in 1999, there is so much more work to do. Inside and outside of academia,

> the language, discourse, and framing of responses to Indigenous rights continue to be fraught with colonizer/settler anxieties and privilege dominating what it means to implement agenda for indigenization or decolonization, reconciliation or recognition. These potentially radical gestures of recognition when implemented can end up as mealy mouthed, watered-down liberal devices that end up reinforcing the status quo. . . . Decolonizing methodologies are about forcing us to confront the Western academic canon in its entirety, in its philosophy, pedagogy, ethics, organizational practices, paradigms, methodologies, and discourses and, important, its self-generating arrogance, its origin mythologies and the stories that it tells to reinforce its hegemony. (xii)

In contrast to the colonial ways of knowing and doing, decolonized research and pedagogical practices are about imagining new ways forward, in which we "work with colonial and Indigenous concepts of knowledge, decentring one while centring the other" (xii).

There are many paths for doing this work, and some of the most powerful guidance Smith provided in the first edition was the imagining of twenty-five possible routes for research and descriptions of what those many avenues might entail. Based on the work of Indigenous scholars around the world, the third edition provides an additional twenty-five projects that demonstrate what decolonizing research can look like. Smith observes that not all of these projects are by Indigenous peoples; there is room for good relationships to be built and ethical work to be done by all.

But sometimes we begin to take for granted what we think we know, and there are moments of transformation when a different community and a different land can remind us of our ignorance and offer us new teachings. I began to learn this in earnest when I moved away from the land I grew up on in the US Midwest and instead lived for a time on the island of O'ahu, part of the Kingdom of Hawai'i. I was an outsider to that land, a guest with a great deal to learn, and these are teachings I have carried with me to southern Appalachia and that I know resonate elsewhere. As a result, for me, Haunani-Kay Trask's legacy has also been powerfully influential. As a leader of the Native Hawaiian sovereignty movement, Trask (may she rest in power) has repeatedly offered a searing indictment of colonial power and reassertion of sovereignty (see *From a Native Daughter: Colonialism and Sovereignty in Hawai'i*). Hers is a vision based on the history and specificity of Hawai'i rather than on those of Indigenous nations on Turtle Island, and this underscores for me the specificity of each Indigenous nation's needs, even as there are some commonalities in experiences under colonialism. Any work that claims to be decolonial or decolonizing in nature must be grounded in the needs of those Indigenous peoples linked to that land (whether that link is current presence or historical connection disrupted because of removal or genocide). Trask's legacy sets an example for pushing back against colonizing narratives of place and the naturalization of colonization, and illuminates her power in calling people to account to work with Native Hawaiian communities rather than claim "local" identity no matter how they or their ancestors arrived on the Hawaiian islands.

One of the key things these elders and ancestors have repeatedly asserted is the necessity of working in relationship to place and positionality. Smith writes from her position as a Māori scholar in Aotearoa/New Zealand, and Trask and Kauanui write from their positions as Kanaka Maoli scholars in Hawai'i. No matter where we are, we need to work with and through and according to our relationships to place.

WHAT DECOLONIALITY AND DECOLONIZATION MEAN TO US ON TURTLE ISLAND

Both of us can recall our early careers as teachers and researchers attempting to decolonize our classroom by teaching Thomas King, asking students to research whose land they are on, or offering an Indigenous practice like making a corn husk doll. Those practices feel like what the thinkers discussed in the previous section are demanding, which is to unsettle and disrupt the traditions of academia, to point to those traditions as Eurocentered and make Indigenous knowledges visible by marking them as intellectual contributions.

But those thinkers do not wholly reflect the experiences of Tribal Nations people of Turtle Island whose land is still occupied by settlers, where the settler project most days feels like it succeeded in wiping us out of every cultural memory through K–12 curricula. Also, we are wholly aware of the ongoing efforts by Indigenous people that can be traced from the very beginning of colonization. To tell the story of decolonization on Turtle Island is to tell it through the Native rhetorics triad of space, culture, and body (Davis). It is to pay attention to land bases and waterways, time, and culture in cyclical and nonlinear ways. We understand decolonization as the active and ongoing process of engaging in Indigenous cultural continuance. Drawing from Qwo-Li Driskill's definition, it is the importance of asserting sovereignty and self-determination and demanding repatriation of Indigenous land and life (69). And drawing on both the Native rhetorics triad (Davis) and Driskill's description of decolonization offers us a way to pinpoint exactly the relationship between epistemic disobedience and reconstruction, as well as the actual movements of sovereignty and self-determination. For us this answers the call and responses to Tuck and Yang's article, "Decolonization Is Not a Metaphor," which addresses both the harms and the missteps of academia and organizing, activist, and professional spaces through its insistence that one cannot invoke decolonization or decoloniality to address antiracism or critical race theory. For Andrea, this shift comes from reading Tuck and Yang's work as well as from deeply understanding the early postco/decolonial theorists who were always writing about their homeland and their connection with knowledge as a way to truly equip themselves with the tools and tactics of resistance and reclamation. These are interconnected and one needs to do both. To write about decolonization on Turtle Island, then, can shift the timeline of when decolonization occurred. We would argue that our ancestors have been engaging in decolonization since the very beginning of colonialism. This could be felt through early forms of resistance such as literally killing French fur traders, intermarriage, and the nineteenth-century survivance practices of Andrew Blackbird, Charles Eastman, and Sarah Winnemuca Hopkins. It could be through witnessing relatives and ancestors fight for treaty rights, the American Indian Religious Freedom Act, and body sovereignty in the 1950s through 1990s.

Tribal Nations people on Turtle Island may not have read Tuck and Yang, or we did but we already lived and experienced both the impacts of settler colonialism and resistance efforts. Our communities, elders, and knowledge keepers have been calling for land repatriation and the ongoing relationship between cultural continuance, survivance, and land since the French and British realized that we were more than opportune traders for peltries. When Andrea thinks about the Tuck and Yang piece, she reads it as a careful and exhaustive intervention on how academia is appropriating decolonial theory to create a new academic field of interest on the backs of Indigenous grassroots organizers fighting for their land and defending Indigenous lives. She appreciates that piece because academia needs an intervention on how we understand decolonial theory and needs to be held accountable for furthering colonial rhetorical practices and not being in relation with Indigenous people. Relying on ancestral, land-based knowledge, Leanne Simpson addresses this disconnect through theorizing that Anishinaabeg knowledge sharing is always pedagogical, consensual, and land based and that academic approaches to education are overt practices of coercion and authority. “Like governance, leadership and every other aspect of reciprocated life, education comes from the roots up. . . . You can’t graduate from Nishnaabewin; it is a gift to be practiced and reproduced” (9). For us, this collection continues and builds on these beliefs: to commit to Indigenous repatriation of land and life while being the arms of the institution is to reorient and recast how we understand learning and doing. It is to prioritize Indigenous communities over the institution. We hope that this collection provides some pathways for this practice.

When Lisa thinks about the Tuck and Yang article, she feels the strength of the indictment of academia, of progressive scholars who want to do good but indiscriminately take up a "cause" without fully understanding what it is or what it means. In addition to their calling out settler moves to innocence, she's struck by Tuck and Yang's assertion of incommensurability, of the need to build coalitions but not concede protected borders that make decolonial work distinct from other also-important movements toward racial justice, against violence against women, girls, and LGBTQTwoSpirit+ folks, and more.

Here's a story Lisa likes to tell that's a metaphor but isn't really: Imagine a single Indigenous mound, a beautiful green bubble of earth several meters high and more than a thousand years old, with a basswood, a white oak, and a sassafras tree growing from it as a naturally seeded trio of guardians. Imagine a small native-plants medicinal garden, a few decades old, holding space on the mound's west side. Imagine the east and north boundaries sharply cutting the green reach of the mound's circumference into a tidy corner with the intersection of two streets and a stoplight; imagine the south side is an enormous parking lot. And then imagine on the north side, just across the street, is an active construction zone. The medicinal garden has some signage that explains the university's work—yes, this is a university campus—to "preserve" and label this space, and in passing the nearest Tribal Nation is mentioned as an influence on the space; look, there's a circle of benches with the official seal of that Indigenous nation where its center fire would be, its opening facing east toward the mound.

This could be a space of tranquility, of endurance, of Indigenous survivance, and it is. Even with the close boundaries of streets and parking and buildings so near, the mound remains. Lisa can take her class to the garden next to the mound and sometimes teach in this space under the shade of dogwood and oak and red cedar, with the official seal of the Eastern Band of Cherokee Indians right in front of her. But she also contends with the noise of traffic and the construction zone (the university's latest evidence of "progress"). The roar of diesel engines, the ground-vibrating thump of digging and driving into the earth, and the metallic screech of heavy construction equipment competes with any attempts to ground visitors to place. As Lisa has told Andrea, "I have literally found myself shouting to be heard."

The mound is not a metaphor. It teaches us that what goes on around our place reflects actual institutional practice and reflects the beliefs and practices of the neoliberal university that strives for modernity and industry but still craves the ancient claim to place. While some good intentions have resulted in limited protection for the mound, the fact is that the day-to-day practices of the institution too often leave the mound neglected, vulnerable, and, in places, literally eroding.

Decolonial spaces may be difficult to make and hold, and the pain and tension of doing so is real; to unsettle academia is the goal. As Simpson writes, "If we accept colonial permanence, then our rebellion can only take place within settler colonial thought and reality; we become too willing to sacrifice the context that creates and produces cultural workers like Kwezens" (8). Reader, as you dwell with us in this introduction and chapters, we hope you understand that our goal is to engage with Simpson's logic while also examining how to reorient ourselves when the colonial noise distracts or disorients us.

SETTLER HARM REDUCTION AND MOVES TO INNOCENCE

Whether engaging with on-the-ground movements or within academia, Indigenous people continue to grapple with the roles of settlers and decoloniality. As members of the CCCC American Indian Caucus, we are part of a long tradition of allowing settlers into the caucus. For us, this practice comes from our caucus elders' decisions to practice kinship and belonging through relational accountability, respect, and reciprocity. We made the decision to practice that relational approach by selectively inviting some settlers into this collection who have demonstrated their consistent commitment to this caucus and local Indigenous groups through their writing and research. What follows is an examination of the work settlers need to do if they want to be in solidarity and kinship with Indigenous communities.

In "Decolonization Is Not a Metaphor," Tuck and Yang define a *settler* as someone coming with the intention of enacting homesteading views, disappearing Indigenous people, and seeking to exert domination. What complicates the presence of settlers is that there are additional experiences of settlement, immigration, and diaspora interconnected with external colonialism. Immigration is a historically and culturally situated experience based on time, culture, bodies, and policy. The story of 1441, when Tristão and Gonçalves took the first West Africans as slaves, is not the story of the Jamestown Colony of 1607. It is not the story of 1619 with the coming of a British slave ship to Jamestown. It is not the story of the flood of German, Irish, and Italian immigrants of the 1850s or the Chinese Exclusion Act of 1882. It is not the story of immigration during World War II or after. It is not the story of Iranian, Iraqian, and Southwest Asian and North African (SWANA) peoples from the 1950s to 1980s or South Americans seeking refugee status today. Where we are definitely not a nation of immigrants, we would argue we are a nation built on stolen land by stolen bodies. As Tuck and Yang describe,

> colonial subjects who are displaced by external colonialism, as well as racialized and minoritized by internal colonialism, still occupy and settle stolen Indigenous land. Settlers are diverse, not just of white European descent, and include people of color, even from other colonial contexts. This tightly wound set of conditions and racialized, globalized relations exponentially complicates what is meant by decolonization, and by solidarity, against settler colonial forces. (6)

In all honesty, it's painful and damn hard to address the topic of privilege, complicity, and beneficiaries of stolen land and settler colonialism with people of color. Whether our ancestors, relatives, and past kin have found themselves on Turtle Island because they were stolen, kidnapped, or entered willingly and then experienced exploitation or systematic incarceration, the reality is that generations later non-Indigenous people on Turtle Island, whether they understand their Indigenous identity from elsewhere or not, are living on stolen Indigenous territories.

We can't erase how this situation came to be, but we can be cautious, careful, intentional, and understanding about how past circumstances lead to present events and, hopefully, liberatory futures. As Tiffany Lethabo King observes, we need another map—another critical formation to understand this complexity:

> I offer the space of the shoal as simultaneously land and sea to fracture this notion that Black diaspora studies is overdetermined by rootlessness and only metaphorized by water and to disrupt the idea that Indigenous studies is solely rooted and fixed in imaginaries of land as territory. . . . The shoal creates a rupture and at the same time opens up analytical possibilities for thinking about Blackness as exceeding the metaphors and analytics of water and for thinking of Indigeneity as exceeding the symbol and analytic of land. (4)

Like decoloniality, we make space for the constellation of experiences regarding how people came here, why their relatives stayed, and what they are doing now to acknowledge what it means to be a visitor on Indigenous land.

Moving forward, we think there are more approaches to demonstrating solidarity and acknowledgment than decoloniality, including addressing settler privilege and complicity, truth (then) reconciliation, settler harm reduction, and abolition. While working with industry and nonprofit organizations, Andrea has led groups through these different movements to help them understand that decoloniality is about options and possibilities and that we all have our own work to do. While we might feel pressure to begin with decoloniality, we encourage folks to do their own work and refrain from assigning someone to something that feels new and exciting just because it is new to them. Although this tactic may demonstrate the appearance of being self-sufficient, instead it is staking a claim on territory where people are already living and doing that work together and in community. In other words, we are drawing attention to how exploration of new ideas and individuality can be interconnected to become a homesteading practice that reifies settler colonialism. Yet we consider this challenge as an opening to navigate the nuance of community boundaries and relationship building.

Although our collective society may have experience with language involved in addressing race, identity, and antiracist logics, that same language is not accessible or embedded in our society regarding settler colonialism. And though we should not use decolonization as a metaphor for social justice, we can look to social justice and antiracist practices to guide settlers, immigrants, and descendants in addressing privilege, complicity, and roles and responsibilities. Tuck and Yang argue that there is no place for settlers in decolonial movements because of settler moves to claim innocence and naivete—in other words, the beliefs and practices settlers employ to diminish their privilege and complicity in settler colonialism and to undermine Indigenous efforts. That doesn't mean there is no work for settlers to do. To be direct, we are shifting how we approach the discourse around decolonization and decoloniality, arguing that it should be an "and" approach and not an "or": we want to make space for *and* protect the frame of decoloniality for Indigenous peoples while showing that there are possibilities for coalition and settler harm reduction.

Before marking your work as decolonial, we encourage readers to understand how they benefit, contribute to, and sustain the colonial matrix of power. What actions, beliefs, and practices do you consciously and unconsciously hold, sustain, and profit from? How do these beliefs and practices take place in your research, writing, and service work? What challenges may occur while working toward Indigenous sovereignty and cultural continuance? Are you prepared and willing to put your job and national reputation at risk to do decolonial work—to side with Tribal Nations people and our collective movements? We encourage readers, all of us, to understand how we are complicit in settler colonialism and serve as the arms of an institution.

This is where our beliefs around decolonization as metaphor are so crucial. You could truly love the idea of epistemic disobedience and write about it for an academic article, but if you are not actually doing the hard work of supporting Indigenous sovereignty and cultural continuance from whatever subject position you claim, you are still committing harm and engaging in cultural appropriation and the conquest of Indigenous knowledges.

Maybe you're reading this and wondering if you're ready to engage with a collection on decolonial theory and practice. We've intentionally designed this collection to make visible the complexities, contradictions, and challenges of doing decolonial work in higher education—even as we, Indigenous people, are complicit in settler colonialism and must negotiate settler colonial expectations in our institutions.

DECOLONIAL THEORY AND INSTITUTIONS

Institutions are hard to deal with; we know from critical race theory (Bell; Crenshaw; Crenshaw et al.; Gillborn and Ladson-Billings; Ladson-Billings and Tate) that our current institutions were built with white supremacy as their foundation and that they function best for white, straight, cisgendered, male-embodied people of European descent. Simply making superficial changes or adding a program here or there won't likely fundamentally change the larger structure, which is why we must always be interrogating our institutions and our positions within them. And as we've already mentioned, it's tempting to fold decolonial and decolonizing work into overlapping discussions of social injustices and think of it as simply another kind of social justice work.

These observations lead us to two questions: How do we make sense of trying to do this kind of work in a university setting (which is just about as institutional as institutions get)? And how do we recognize similarly minded and related movements and build good coalitions without losing sight of what decolonizing work is?

As we've observed, academia is like kudzu that grows right over indigenous plants to extract what it needs and position itself to get the best light and resources. It's a hardy plant, and there are things to admire about it so long as it remains in balance with others. Its strengths make it an invasive and destructive species, though, when it is allowed to grow uncontrolled outside of its kin network. Similarly, colleges and universities can be sites for growth and innovation and new ways of being and thinking, but we cannot ignore that they were designed and tend to still propagate only specific kinds of Eurocentric knowledges based on a system of values that emphasizes competition and domination as key values. And before anyone challenges the kudzu metaphor with some "survival of the fittest" nonsense, Western science is beginning to understand with traditional ecological knowledges (TEK) from Indigenous peoples that there is plenty to be said about how plants and animals don't actually act ruthlessly but instead rather frequently in terms of community and resource sharing (Kimmerer). Likewise, our educational institutions need to be reoriented and redesigned. But in the meantime, we can use the power we have to hold space. In a garden, that means cutting the invasive species back and removing them, or at the very least trying to reduce their harm and to hold space for indigenous species to flourish again.

In less metaphorical terms, it means cutting back the narratives of "progress" and instead "telling the hard truths of colonization" as part of our work. In her work on museums, a related kind of educational institution and one that frequently dovetails with universities, Amy Lonetree argues that decolonizing museums "must involve assisting our [Native and Indigenous] communities in addressing the legacies of historical unresolved grief. Doing this necessarily cuts through the veil of silence around colonialism and its consequences for Native families and communities" (5). While she is speaking primarily of Tribal museums here, all of our educational institutions need to do this work.

Why not burn it all down instead? As legitimate as that temptation might feel sometimes, and unless you all want to help us get some gasoline, we want to use this collection to run interventions and hold space within our educational systems, not the least because

1. Educational institutions are established sites of power, and leaving them unchecked does more harm than good;

2. Educational institutions are built on and (with the Morrill Act) with the sale of Indigenous lands (Lee and Ahtone), and so have a responsibility;
3. We have Indigenous students, whether we "see" them or not, and they are just as deserving of support;
4. Systemic change happens with a critical mass of like-minded people, and the college or university is one of the few places we have where non-Indigenous students have the chance to hear these histories for the first time and think through their connections with them; and
5. Rhetoric and writing studies has a particular stake in this because of its developing desire to question and intervene in our understandings of language and communicating, and its connection and relationship building within and across communities, in terms of past, present, and future.

CONNECTED AND COALIGNED WITHOUT LOSING THE DIFFERENCE

We've mentioned through our discussion of Tuck and Yang that decolonization is not just another kind of antiracist or social justice work. Like countless grassroots movements, decolonization is part of a cross-coalition effort to not appropriate a movement and set of knowledge practices but to understand particular struggles and forms of activism within a cultural context. As we've always understood, whether from Black Lives Matter, LGBTQ+, disabled, or immigrant groups, Indigenous people share these subject identities and so there are important forms of cross-coalitional possibilities. In other words, to do decolonial work is to not exist in a vacuum of precontact Turtle Island. Instead, it is to understand that to engage in decoloniality, decolonial theory and practice, and decolonial possibilities is to be committed to Indigenous lived experiences, sovereignty, and cultural continuance. This collection guides you on how to do this while also understanding how decolonial practice and theory are interconnected with constellations of antiracist and social justice paradigms and practices.

In particular, the relationships between Black and Indigenous communities and peoples deserve attention. As is well documented, the United States is a country built on stolen Indigenous land and built with stolen Black labor. It is also a country in which racial hierarchies imported from Europe took root: in which sometimes Indigenous peoples were ranked as "colored" and therefore found themselves allied alongside Black communities, or alternatively were ranked higher than Black people and as a result were afforded some recognition by settlers for playing by that hierarchy (Miles). At some times and places, Indigenous peoples were enslaved; in others, they were the enslavers. At some times and places, Indigenous and Black peoples worked together, intermarried, and fought side by side. At other times, they did not.

These histories are tangled, and painful. Anti-Indigenous sentiment exists in Black communities as elsewhere in the bid to be more acceptable on whitestream terms, and anti-Black sentiment exists in Indigenous communities and nations today (perhaps the best-known example is the case of the Cherokee Freedmen). But we also have some powerful opportunities to build on the successful alliances of the past and strengthen those of the present. As Tiya Miles and Sharon P. Holland ask,

> What happens when key issues in African diasporic experience, such as migration, freedom, citizenship, belonging, peoplehood, and cultural retention and creation, and key issues in Native American experience, such as tribalism, protection of homelands, self-determination, political sovereignty, and cultural-spiritual preservation and renewal, converge? (4)

Put more in the terms of our field, what happens when the rhetorical traditions of each of these communities meet and intersect on these topics? Or put another way, if "Black belonging and Indigenous survivance remains central to how they have survived and continue to do so into the future" (Mays xxiii), how do we understand the complex constellation of desires, rhetorical strategies and approaches, and intentions and effects of Black belonging and Indigenous survivance as they meet, particularly with the different-but-related-through-colonialism goals of social justice and decolonization? Kyle Mays directly suggests that "[p]eople of African descent have a responsibility to think about their relationship to this indigenous [sic] place, and what their responsibility might be going forward to Indigenous nations. By the same token, Indigenous people of what is now the United States . . . have a responsibility to their Black relatives" (xxii). Particularly to that last point, there are family legacies that include both Black and Indigenous identities, and for these individuals and communities, what might social justice and decolonization mean? We have so much work to do.

While our goals for this collection mean keeping the focus primarily on the Indigenous peoples of Turtle Island, we are well aware that coalition building is also incredibly important so long as the goals and procedures mean everyone's goals and needs are being met. It makes no sense to raise one community at the expense of another, and yet often it can be incredibly difficult to find ways to build connection when our energies are consumed with the work within our own communities. We recognized even as we put this collection together that talking through the rhetorics of Black and Indigenous decolonial relationships is a gap in Indigenous rhetorics scholarship, pointing toward work that needs to be taken up.

Though it is beyond the scope of this collection to talk through in detail what that coalition building across all possible communities might look like, we want to acknowledge the recent work in our field across CCCC caucuses and the promise that new work holds to show us a way toward coalition work that lifts everyone without erasing our different goals. The seeds are planted; we hope that this collection can contribute to growth.

TRUTH AND RECONCILIATION

If we are thinking about decolonized and Indigenous futures, what of reconciliation? It should go without saying that reconciliation can't happen until the hard truths have been spoken and changes have been made, to not just apologize for but tangibly make efforts to unsettle the structures we take for granted. Otherwise, "conciliatory" acts become acts of violence.

I (Lisa) share this story to help explain. When I was preparing to visit the Saginaw Chippewa Indian Tribe of Michigan's Ziibiwing

Center while they were preparing to host the *Walking with Our Sisters* memorial in 2016 (http://walkingwithoursisters.ca/), I was invited to be a volunteer to help with the installation. This installation of moccasin vamps and ceremonial objects was a traveling space/event that changed its shaped each time according to the needs of the host community, but what never changed was the understanding that this memorial was a sacred space for remembering and mourning, and for building awareness around the violence that colonial systems (particularly law enforcement) enacted and enact every time an Indigenous woman or child goes missing or murdered. These women and children were murdered and missing in part because colonial law enforcement either did not do its job in solving these cases or, in some instances, was the perpetrator itself. Visitors were required to remove their shoes to enter the space, photography was forbidden after the ceremonial opening, and visitors were asked to respectfully use the space for quiet contemplation. Such a space could hypothetically be a way to start the conversation around how healing might happen and in turn encourage some kind of reconciliation.

Yet one of the most striking moments for me was bearing witness to a moment on the first day of the installation's opening when the media and local non-Tribal law enforcement arrived to see the space. The police officers were in full uniform, armed, with handcuffs and weapons visible on their belts. The women elders caring for the space stopped them as they were removing their shoes: "You can't go in like that. Yes, you took your shoes off, but you are still going into this space wearing the uniform of the people and systems who participated in this violence that we bear witness to. We need you to go home and change your clothes. Come back and bear witness as a human being, not as a police officer."

There was a tense moment when the police officers regarded the elders; it was clear that the officers were debating whether to take offense, because after all, weren't they doing Indigenous folks a favor by even showing up? But then they quietly backed down, put their shoes back on, and left. I don't know whether they came back; many visitors came through that day, and the next, and if they did return, I didn't notice them specifically because they didn't present themselves in the uniforms of colonial power and instead came back as humans.

This story illustrates the difference between trying to enact reconciliation on the colonial structure's terms and enacting it on Indigenous communities' terms. As Andrea V. Breen and colleagues observe in their introduction to *Research and Reconciliation: Unsettling Ways of Knowing through Indigenous Relationships*, reconciliation and healing don't happen if folks are "box-tickers engaging in bullshit ways" or "appropriating concepts like Indigenization and reconciliation for their own purposes" (xiv), or if reconciliation is equated with "saving Indigenous people" or "used as a shield, like a protective armor of good intentions, when the work that is being done isn't always different from other ugly things that came before" (xiii). And like the concepts of sovereignty or decolonization, reconciliation has to be defined within the needs and contexts of Indigenous nations and communities, not by the colonial institution calling the shots. Just taking your shoes off isn't enough; divesting yourself of the accoutrements of violence is the first actual step. Breen et al. accordingly refuse to offer a definitive breakdown of what reconciliation is and instead observe that it can be "attempts to improve social relations between Indigenous and non-Indigenous peoples; . . . specific calls to action and processes outlined by national governments; . . . healing within our families and communities; . . . [and a process] within ourselves" (xi). Part of the work that precedes and constitutes any move to reconciliation is therefore putting the locally defined work of decolonization into practice.

KNOWING WHERE WE ARE, OUR LIMITATIONS, OUR POSSIBILITIES

Currently, we are on different territories. Andrea, on the ancestral territory of the Anishinaabeg, and Lisa on Aniyunwiya (Cherokee) territories that also connect to Muscogean, Yuchi, Coushatta, and Shawnee peoples. Both of us are navigating institutional and community expectations while trying to make Indigenous space, engage with Indigenous students, and educate settlers. These territories, their histories, and the communities still there guide our work, our relationships with our institutions, and our efforts to engage students.

We decided to take up this collection partly to grapple with the complexities, contradictions, and pleasure and grief that come with decolonial work and to think through what an honest reckoning would look like, from publishing and research practices to infrastructure and administration all the way to daily classroom practices. That kind of project is truthfully beyond the scope of a single edited collection, but in community with our contributors we do offer here a series of reflections and analyses of what decolonial and decolonizing work is on the ground, what we've tried, the institutional pushback or inertia we've encountered, the successes we've had, and the challenges we've faced. There is no single blanket solution for how to decolonize academia. In fact, we have debated with each other what decoloniality could and should mean. We've agreed and disagreed depending on how the week went, including interactions with Indigenous community members, working with students, or mentoring colleagues. Some might even argue that it can't be done at all insofar as academia was designed, developed, and deployed to be a colonizing force and still is. As Patrick Wolfe famously observed, settler colonialism is a structure, not a one-off, single-moment-in-time event.

At the same time, we reject the notion that nothing at all can be done. We are guided by the belief that we have a responsibility to try to do something. After all, with every Indigenous studies course, land acknowledgment, settler harm reduction training, Indigenous leadership camp, or culturally responsive museum exhibition, another Indigenous student remains in academia and engages with their cultural and educational journey. We do have agency, those of us who are Indigenous and those who are coconspirators/allies, and we can definitely call out institutional violence, uproot colonial structures, reduce settler harm, and hold space for Indigenous ways of knowing and being. Big changes come from small changes, after all.

You'll also observe how the COVID-19 pandemic is now threaded through much of our work; we took this project up in the fall of 2019 and submitted the original proposal in January 2020, not knowing what the next years would bring. As others have amply documented and as every person on Turtle Island has felt, the pandemic exposed the cracks and chasms of inequity in our (colonial, neoliberal, capitalism-driven) educational system, and we watched and suffered as administrators and institutions made destructive choices that put the most vulnerable at risk. Even as we wrote this introduction, the pandemic was still happening. Andrea was recovering from COVID and was grateful to be vaccinated. Lisa was managing the conservative "divisive concepts" laws established in her community that put her and her family at risk. This meant that to honor the needs of our contributors (and, frankly, ourselves), we slowed the pace of the project down to give everyone the time to process and write. We intended this slowdown as a decolonial act of resistance; rather than produce at the cost of our bodies, our families, and our communities, we remembered how Indigenous communities have survived epidemic illness before us—by caring for one another—and this project was completed along those lines and no others.

Far from missing our moment of exigence, however, the urgent need to address our fields remains. As work on antiracism in the academy gains momentum, now more than ever we need to address the erasure of Indigenous rhetorics and peoples and anti-Indigeneity because they are attached to the colonial structures that also produced racial constructs and harmed people-of-color (POC) communities. This is all connected.

OVERVIEW OF CHAPTERS

Since our intention is to identify both decolonial possibilities and gaps in current scholarly conversations, each contributor provides their experiences, successes, challenges, and ongoing goals. These chapters provide both framework and practice, serving as models to inspire the energy to develop new projects as well as return to ongoing work from a decolonial perspective. For some contributors,

Indigenous presence is strong and the institutions they operate in are open to decolonial options; for others, their institutions may do nothing at all, and creating and holding Indigenous space has to begin with institutional critique. Indigenizing the academy and decolonial work depend on both institutions and relationships with Indigenous communities. Regardless of where each contributor finds themselves, we hope that you will be able to identify decolonial possibilities wherever you are situated as we invite you into the circle and into the conversation. We also recognize that we cannot cover all of Turtle Island, and that what we offer here very much reflects the relationships, connections, and placement of our contributors. But the work to be done extends all over the continent, from the largest federally recognized Tribe (the Navajo Nation) to smaller state recognized Tribes, from reservations to urban centers, and every educational institution in between.

We chose to begin with a foreword by Malea Powell, who offers elder teachings for both BIPOC and European Americans. In many ways, this collection picks up the threads from previous work in Lisa's *Survivance, Sovereignty, and Story*, but this time with a more explicit decolonial orientation in talking about Indigenous rhetorics and practices in curricula and in the classroom. As editors we recognize that curriculum development and teaching are often the first places individual instructors, no matter their rank, can make an intervention, and so these chapters offer more ideas for teaching.

Kimberly Wieser-Weryackwe offers one approach in Chapter 1, "Takissaawoo': Indigenous Practices of Visiting as Pedagogical Praxis." She articulates a culture-brokering, nonlinear, narrative-based pedagogy that encourages students to learn and practice skills in empathy, interpersonal communication, and diplomacy as they absorb course content through story. Her approach is based on the Blackfoot custom of Takissaawoo', or visiting, which allows class members to develop relationships and a sense of community. Wieser-Weryackwe examines the sources of this visiting practice, which has equivalents in most Indigenous cultures, and offers information on how these elements can be replicated, thus decolonizing the classroom.

Chapter 2, "Building Relationships as a Way to Engage in Decolonial Practice," articulates the ways in which Yavanna M. Brownlee moves beyond the social justice efforts we might be accustomed to hearing about in the classroom and grounds her pedagogy more explicitly in Indigenous decolonial practices. While challenging systemic racism, heteropatriarchy, and white privilege is important, those challenges are not decolonizing until they are linked explicitly to settler colonialism and the histories and needs of Indigenous nations and peoples. Helping students parse out these relational constellations and locate themselves within them can be a powerful decolonizing pedagogical approach.

Reconceptualizing classroom relationships is also part of the work that Catheryn Jennings does in Chapter 3, "Decolonial Practice as a Path for Community Kindness in the Classroom." Directly addressing the intersection of circumstances in her classroom—the first full semester of the COVID-19 pandemic, the pivot to online teaching, and her first semester as an assistant professor—Jennings reflects on how "radical kindness" is part of decolonial classroom practice. Prioritizing relationality and Indigenous knowledge-making practices in the classroom reveals how the pandemic simply made more visible the problems of a settler-colonial classroom, and how decolonizing in this way is both a challenge and mutually beneficial for students and instructors.

In the final chapter discussing pedagogy specifically, Jaquetta Shade-Johnson points us toward another way of embodying decolonial practices in the classroom. Chapter 4, "Engaging Native Land and Indigenous Food Sovereignty in a Food Writing Classroom: A Decolonizing Pedagogical Practice," explores how food sovereignty can play a role in establishing connections between students and land-based relationships. Through an Indigenous rhetorics and cultural rhetorics approach, Shade-Johnson discusses how her special-topics food writing course became a space in which to understand the power dynamics of history, its colonial impact, and the decolonizing efforts of contemporary Native American professionals who act on behalf of their own communities. More important, she argues, students' growing understanding of

Indigenous foodways and reciprocal relationships with the land encourages them to better understand the social injustices woven through their own food systems and to address them.

But as any reader will know, mentoring is also a key part of academic labor that opens doors and makes connected research possible. Cindy Tekobbe takes up the relational potential of mentoring relationships in Chapter 5, "Tending the Fire: Graduate Mentoring as Decolonial Practice," outlining a decolonial approach to mentoring graduate students that focuses on three basic strategies: checking in, listening, and celebrating. After her own graduate school and early professional experiences of attempting to achieve a work-life balance left her feeling torn between focusing solely on her writing and research or maintaining inclusive relationships among colleagues, friends, and family members, Tekobbe developed and refined this approach and offers it here as an example of decolonial thinking. Moving away from the colonialist notion that faculty can't and shouldn't "solve their [students'] problems," Tekobbe outlines for mentors a relational, Indigenous approach to inclusion that practices and maintains active inclusion, affirmation, normalization, and support.

Given that rhetoric and composition as a field often grounds itself in writing programs and writing centers as part of its institutional home, we have a chapter on writing center work and how it connects to decolonial possibilities. In Chapter 6, "A Writing Center's Place Is in the #Community: Decolonizing Writing Center Administration," Deidre Anne Evans Garriott argues that many writing center best practices—among both consultants and administrators—are deeply wedded to and rely on colonial practices that write over and subsume writers and the knowledge they bring to the academy. She also notes research indicating that writing centers are not "safe spaces" as imagined by those who are deeply embedded in contemporary colonialist approaches to writing and assistance with writing. Pointing to the inherent racisms continuing to dominate such academic locations, Garriott explores decolonialized writing center practices by reorienting the identities of writing center workers, particularly administrators, as accomplices rather than protectors of (so-called) safe spaces, and uses her own institution as a place to begin questioning how that might change.

Chapter 7, "Invisibility and Colonial Logics: Narrative Reframing of Indigenous Presence on Campus," offers a kind of case study of a large land-grant institution and the kinds of decolonial possibilities that can be identified. Lisa King's contribution reinforces that contemporary university settings are still predominantly oriented toward westernized ways of knowing, which does not accept and honor Indigenous epistemologies. She seeks to illuminate these misguided assumptions and the institutions that further them, following a method established by the Reclaiming Native Truth project. Focusing on her own institution, King identifies the lack of Indigenous visibility at the University of Tennessee, Knoxville, identifies student and campus narratives erasing Indigenous presences, reframes such stories, and provides a model for strategic delinking from such colonial logics.

Luhui Whitebear offers her reflections through the multiple roles she occupies at Oregon State University, a predominantly white institution (PWI)—as a PhD student, as director of the Native American Longhouse (NAL) Eena Haws at OSU, as an instructor of undergraduates, and as an Indigenous woman of color on her campus—in Chapter 8, "A Story of Parallel Worlds: Decolonial Possibilities Navigating Institutional Spaces." Whether it is defining Indigenous identity, developing land acknowledgments with local Indigenous communities, or Indigenizing the classroom, Whitebear demonstrates the many ways she must negotiate the power structures of an institution that was not built with Indigenous people in mind, providing a glimpse into what can be done and what must still be done on her campus.

Institutional change does not only mean examining individual campuses; it means examining other kinds of academic infrastructure. In Chapter 9, "On Embodied Rhetorical Choices; or, Cultivating a Decolonial Approach to Publishing," Christina V. Cedillo describes the field of publishing and its colonial influence on Indigenous epistemologies, which perpetuate biases against people of color.

Based on her experience editing an online, open-access journal, she offers advice to editors for decolonizing their own practices—recommending that editors assume the role of collaborators dependent on the contexts and purposes of authors. Using a Coatlicue perspective, Cedillo argues "that the backgrounding of publication work ties directly to the backgrounding of Othered voices and that transformation of our discipline requires that we demystify the publication process, thereby rendering it open to critique and change." Coatlicue, the mother of the Mexica war god Huitzilopochtli, serves as a figure that can represent resistance to Eurocentric culture and colonial patriarchy. Drawing from her experiences as editor of the *Journal of Multimodal Rhetorics*, Cedillo explains the guiding principles of *JOMR* and its relationship to decolonial thinking.

We conclude with a recorded conversation titled "Making Indigenous Space through Anishinaabeg Knowledge and Community Relations" by Belinda (Lin) Bardwell and Andrea Riley Mukavetz, who provide the community and institutional context that informs their work, including community-based research and supporting Indigenous students. Speaking from the perspectives of a staff member who specializes in Native student retention (Belinda) and a faculty member (Andrea), they explore the challenges of Anishinaabeg-consensus approaches to governance and decolonizing higher education environments. At the time of this conversation, Bardwell and Riley Mukavetz were both employed at Grand Valley State University in western Michigan where there is a visible Anishinaabek population that they too are a part of. This conversation provides another layer to understanding the complexities of Indigenizing and decolonizing institutional spaces as Indigenous people who are a part of their communities. Readers can learn from these challenges as well as identify the possibilities for making Indigenous space on college campuses. We offer this discussion as a model for readers to understand how two Anishinaabekwe navigate their relationships with the university while being a part of their community and enacting Anishinaabe teachings.

CONCLUSION

As we bring this introductory arc to its end, we are dwelling with Aunty Malea's foreword. We leave you with a few requests. Go outside wherever you are and touch the earth. Ask yourself, where am I, and what is my relationship to this place? What might my responsibilities be as a good guest and relative to this land's First Nations and to all our relations (water, plant, and animal relatives)? This practice reflects how land-based relationships are central to decolonial possibilities inside and outside of academia. We want to underscore Aunty Malea's entreaty to say the quiet things aloud. For us, this request is a way to take responsibility and intervene in our own complicity in the colonial project of higher education. Perhaps, after reading this collection, you will come away thinking that it's not possible to do decolonial work. If so, that's okay. This work is not for everyone. But we ask that you still find a way to be in relation with us, with the natural world, and with Indigenous communities, including students, faculty, and staff. We ask that you intentionally say the quiet things aloud because that will create space and affirm and care for those of us continuing to be hopeful, continuing to invest in this painful work, continuing to work for the next seven generations.

NOTE

1. It should be acknowledged here that the AIC supports scholars of various Indigenous backgrounds and identities as a way to recognize the complex ways that colonialism and settler colonialism have made a negative impact, drawn artificial boundaries, and disrupted kinship systems and community building. No one here claims enrollment in a Native Nation when they aren't, or makes an essentialist argument based on their DNA, or uses cultural knowledge or language without explaining how they come by it.

WORKS CITED

Bell, Derrick A. David C. Baum Memorial Lecture: "Who's Afraid of Critical Race Theory?" *University of Illinois Law Review*, vol. 4, 1995.

Breen, Andrea V., et al. Introduction. *Research and Reconciliation: Unsettling Ways of Knowing through Indigenous Relationships*, edited by Shawn Wilson et al., Canadian Scholars/CSP Books, 2019.

Brooks, Lisa. *The Common Pot: The Recovery of Native Space in the Northeast.* U of Minnesota P, 2008.

Césaire, Aimé. *Discourse on Colonialism.* 1955. Monthly Review Press, 2000.

Clary-Lemon, Jennifer, and David M. Grant, editors. *Decolonial Conversations in Posthuman and New Material Rhetorics.* Ohio State UP, 2022.

Crenshaw, Kimberlé. "Unmasking Colorblindness in the Law: Lessons from the Formation of Critical Race Theory." *Seeing Race Again: Countering Colorblindness Across the Disciplines*, edited by Kimberlé Williams Crenshaw et al., U of California P, 2019, pp. 52–84.

Crenshaw, Kimberlé, et al., editors. *Critical Race Theory: The Key Writings That Formed the Movement.* The New Press, 1995.

Davis, Andréa D. "Growing Our Discipline: An Interview with Malea Powell." *Composition Forum*, vol. 23, Spring 2011.

Dei, George Sefa. "Indigenous Anti-colonial Knowledge as 'Heritage Knowledge' for Promoting Black/African Education in Diasporic Contexts." *Decolonization: Indigeneity, Education & Society*, vol. 1, no. 1, 2012, pp. 102–19.

Driskill, Qwo-Li. "Doubleweaving Two-Spirit Critiques: Building Alliances between Native and Queer Studies. *GLQ: A Journal of Lesbian and Gay Studies,* vol. 16, no. 1–2, 2010, pp. 69–92.

Fanon, Frantz. *The Wretched of the Earth.* Grove Press, 1961.

García, Romeo, et al., editors. *Pluriversal Literacies: Tools for Perseverance and Livable Futures.* U of Pittsburgh P, 2023.

García, Romeo, and Damián Baca, editors. *Rhetorics Elsewhere and Otherwise: Contested Modernities, Decolonial Visions.* Conference on College Composition and Communication, National Council of Teachers of English, 2019.

Gillborn, David, and Gloria Ladson-Billings. "Critical Race Theory." *SAGE Research Methods Foundations*, edited by Paul Atkinson et al., SAGE Publications, 2019.

Haas, Angela M. "Race, Rhetoric, and Technology: A Case Study of Decolonial Technical Communication Theory, Methodology, and Pedagogy." *Journal of Business and Technical Communication*, vol. 26, no. 3, 2012, pp. 277–310.

Itchuaqiyaq, Cana Uluak. "Iñupiat Ilitqusiat: An Indigenist Ethics Approach for Working with Marginalized Knowledges in Technical Communication." *Equipping Technical Communicators for Social Justice Work: Theories, Methodologies, and Pedagogies,* edited by R. Walton and Godwin Y. Agboka, Utah State UP, 2021, pp. 33–48.

Itchuaqiyaq, Cana Uluak, and Breeanne Matheson. "Decolonizing Decoloniality: Considering the (Mis)use of Decolonial Frameworks in TPC Scholarship." *Communication Design Quarterly*, vol. 9, no. 1, 2021, pp. 20–31.

Kauanui, J Kēhaulani. "'A Structure, Not an Event': Settler Colonialism and Enduring Indigeneity." *Lateral: Journal of the Cultural Studies Association*, vol. 5, no. 1, Spring 2016.

Kimmerer, Robin Wall. *Braiding Sweetgrass: Indigenous Wisdom, Scientific Knowledge, and the Teachings of Plants*. Milkweed Editions, 2013.

King, Lisa, Rose Gubele, and Joyce Rain Anderson, editors. *Survivance, Sovereignty, and Story: Teaching American Indian Rhetorics*. Utah State UP, 2015.

King, Tiffany Lethabo. *The Black Shoals: Offshore Formations of Black and Native Studies*. Duke UP, 2019.

Ladson-Billings, Gloria, and William F. Tate IV. "Toward a Critical Race Theory of Education." *Teachers College Record,* vol. 97, no. 1, 1995, pp. 47–68.

Lee, Robert, and Tristan Ahtone. "Land-Grab Universities." *High Country News*, 30 March 2020, https://www.hcn.org/issues/52.4/indigenous-affairs-education-land-grab-universities.

Lonetree, Amy. *Decolonizing Museums: Representing Native America in National and Tribal Museums*. U of North Carolina P, 2012.

Lyons, Scott Richard. "Rhetorical Sovereignty: What Do American Indians Want from Writing?" *College Composition and Communication,* vol. 51, no. 3, 2000, pp. 447–68.

Mays, Kyle T. *An Afro-Indigenous History of the United States*. Beacon Press, 2021.

Mignolo, Walter D. *The Darker Side of Western Modernity: Global Futures, Decolonial Options*. Duke UP, 2011.

Miles, Tiya. "Dispossession." *The 1619 Project: A New Origin Story*, edited by Nikole Hannah-Jones et al., Random House Large Print, 2021, pp. 135–55.

Miles, Tiya, and Sharon P. Holland. "Introduction: Crossing Waters, Crossing Worlds." *Crossing Waters, Crossing Worlds: The African Diaspora in Indian Country*, edited by Tiya Miles and Sharon P. Holland, Duke UP, 2006, pp. 1–23.

Powell, Malea D. "Blood and Scholarship: One Mixed-Blood's Dilemma." *Race, Rhetoric, and Composition*, edited by Keith Gilyard, Boynton/Cook, pp. 1–16.

———. "Down by the River, or How Susan La Flesche Can Teach Us about Alliance as a Practice of Survivance." *College English,* vol. 67, no. 1, 2004, pp. 38–60.

———. "Rhetorics of Survivance: How American Indians Use Writing." *College Composition and Communication,* vol. 53, no. 3, 2002, pp. 396–434.

Riley Mukavetz, Andrea M. "Towards a Cultural Rhetorics Methodology: Making Research Matter with Multi-Generational Women from the Little Traverse Bay Band." *Journal of Rhetoric, Professional Communication, and Globalization,* vol. 5, no. 1, 2014, p. 109.

Ruiz, Iris D., and Raúl Sánchez, editors. *Decolonizing Rhetoric and Composition Studies: New Latinx Keywords for Theory and Pedagogy.* Palgrave Macmillan, 2016.

Simpson, Leanne Betasamosake. "Land as Pedagogy: Nishnaabeg Intelligence and Rebellious Transformation." *Decolonization: Indigeneity, Education & Society,* vol. 3, no. 3, 2014, pp. 1–25.

Sleeper-Smith, Susan, 'et al., editors. *Why You Can't Teach United States History without American Indians.* U of North Carolina P, 2015.

Smith, Linda Tuhiwai. *Decolonizing Methodologies: Research and Indigenous Peoples.* 3rd ed., Zed Books, 2021.

Thiong'o, Ngugi wa. *Decolonising the Mind: The Politics of Language in African Literature.* East African Educational Publishers, 1992.

Trask, Haunani-Kay. *From a Native Daughter: Colonialism and Sovereignty in Hawai'i.* 2nd ed., Latitude 20 Book, U of Hawai'i P, 1999.

Tuck, Eve, and K. Wayne Yang. "Decolonization Is Not a Metaphor." *Decolonization: Indigeneity, Education & Society,* vol. 1, no. 1, 2012, pp. 1–40.

Walking with Our Sisters. Commemorative Art Installation. Walking with Our Sisters Collective, 2012–2020, http://walkingwithoursisters.ca/.

Wieser, Kimberly G., et al., editors. "American Indian and Indigenous Rhetorics: A Digital Annotated Bibliography." *Journal of Multimodal Rhetorics,* vol. 5, no. 2, Fall 2021.

Wolfe, Patrick. "Settler Colonialism and the Elimination of the Native." *Journal of Genocide Research,* vol. 8, no. 4, 2006, pp. 387–409.

Womack, Craig S. *Red on Red: Native American Literary Separatism.* U of Minnesota P, 1999.

Chapter 1

Takissaawoo': Indigenous Practices of Visiting as Pedagogical Praxis

Kimberly Wieser-Weryackwe
University of Oklahoma

INTRODUCTION

THIS CHAPTER IS A STORY. Like any good story, it is going to take you on a journey. I think it best that I give you a road map—or a story map, if you prefer. First, I'm going to take my writing stick and draw you a picture of where we are going, a guide that shows the road and the "major places"—or big ideas—we are going to visit. Then I am going to put that writing stick in my pack and pick up my walking stick to lead you on that journey, explaining what we see along the way.

In terms of the major places we are going to visit, the big ideas in this chapter are grounded in Blackfoot scholar Leroy Little Bear's Native paradigm of relatedness, respect, reciprocity, and renewal. Along our route, I will tell you about my classroom praxis, a culture-brokering, nonlinear, narrative-based pedagogy. This way of educating teaches students empathy, interpersonal communication skills, and diplomacy as it teaches them course content. This is particularly important in my classrooms in Oklahoma where the state shares space with thirty-nine Tribal nations. My students all need to understand how to work together to make this space a better one for us all and for future generations.

My teaching practice is akin to the Blackfoot custom of Takissaawoo', or "visiting . . . really spending time with each other." Blackfoot people say, "Iiksoka'pii iihkanao'too's"—"it's good we have all come together," with the connotations of *good*, as common in Indigenous languages, being equated with a sense of rightness and balance in mind, heart, body, and spirit, as well as with all of our relations, all of Sacred Creation. This classroom praxis developed organically for me based on my experiences teaching in Indian Country, in particular during a four-year diasporic stint as a professor at the University of Lethbridge in southern Alberta, where Professor Little Bear was my mentor and the vast majority of my mostly Indigenous students were Blackfoot. Takissaawoo' as a practice has its equivalent in all Indigenous cultures and is the medium through which new relationships are developed and community grows.

In our daily lives as humans, as we live, work, create, make, play, and celebrate together, we inevitably impact one another through showing respect or a lack of respect, engaging in reciprocity or in nonreciprocal behaviors, and, from Indigenous perspectives, renewing our relationships of various kinds through daily ritual and prayer, through ceremonies, gifting, and sharing time and meals together, and, most of all, through the communicative, pedagogical, and restorative practice of story. To inform my pedagogical practice, I examine visiting in several contexts in Indigenous culture—social, ceremonial, and diplomatic—to see what elements of these praxes can be incorporated into a more Indigenous classroom praxis in terms of delivery, discussion, and application. Both the protocols that guide our interactions and the pedagogical practices that inform the knowledge transfer, problem solving, making, evaluating, and correcting that take place in my classrooms are shaped by Takissaawoo'. I structure the labor of my teaching with the idea of making the "work" invisible by naturalizing it through the intentional repetition of exposition, story, and dialogue, the components most common in the unconsciously structured discourse of Takissaawoo'.

Learning, in Indigenous cultures, can and does take place within this context, learning that is measured by a very high standard because for Indigenous people the stakes are always survival. Everything we know, every bit of knowledge that is passed on, whether ceremonial or practical, is about the continuance of life.

Learning is always shared survivance. Traditional knowledge and skills are taught by real-life modeling, apprenticeship, practice, and redoing until the product is perfected. As Little Bear teaches, the only passing grade, traditionally speaking, is 100 percent. This kind of teaching is a responsibility taken on when I decide to engage in a more Indigenous pedagogy that requires both me and the students to see our classroom as a space where we can respectfully make and renew reciprocal relationships. From Native perspectives, this kind of practice is healing, is decolonial, for Native and non-Native students alike. For me, story is at the center of this.

WHAT ARE WE HEALING FROM?

> I will tell you something about stories,
> [he said]
> They aren't just entertainment.
> Don't be fooled.
> They are all we have, you see,
> All we have to fight off
> illness and death.
> You don't have anything if you don't have the stories. (Silko 213)

While today we see studies on using the Native practice of story in healing in a variety of societal sectors—historical and contemporary trauma work, medicine, and veterans' programs, for instance—what better place for story than the Native textual studies classrooms within which we teach? After all, Native literature and rhetoric courses are transits from Indian Country to society at large, where story travels the most frequently in the academy, shaping the next generation to influence others.

As one of the purposes of story is to rebalance relationships, it is important to talk about the populations of the classes I have taught through which this pedagogy developed and the issues in both their texts and the world around them that have caused imbalances students feel strongly about addressing in the classroom. My classrooms are still dominated, in Oklahoma at least, by a middle-class, heterosexual, white audience that has lived next to, but not with, Oklahoma's Indigenous population for several generations. Made up typically of anywhere from twenty to thirty students, my classes generally have between three to five American Indian students, one or two Latinx students, and one or two students with Indigenous heritage but without status, in contrast to my classrooms in Lethbridge, where the majority of the students I taught were First Nations, Métis, or Inuit (FNMI). My University of Oklahoma classrooms also usually have a few out-of-state students, mostly from Texas, a few other American students who are POC, several students who are LGBTQ+, and a handful of international students. Together we make meaning of texts and the contemporary and historical reality of Indian Country today. If we can do this while undoing the stereotypes incubated in our young people through the systematic whitewashing of mainstream popular culture and K–12 public education via the hidden curriculum designed to uphold the political mythology of the United States and maintain the status quo, we can hope to reduce racism and hate crimes and promote greater collaboration between Indian and non-Indian people in Okla Humma, leading to better lives for us all.

My Native and Indigenous students here in Oklahoma and the FNMI students I taught during my four years at Lethbridge in Alberta, which has a larger Indigenous population and is just outside the largest Indian reservation in that country, as well as near several smaller ones, have typically wanted to talk about issues that, through study and discussion, could impact positive, decolonizing change for Indigenous people. These issues are what make Indigenous students carry their texts outside of classrooms to family and community, sometimes not getting them back until final exams. Indigenous students want change, change from mainstream America, change from the global community, and change from themselves, their communities, and their loved ones. Indigenous students want to interrogate their grief as it manifests through poverty, gender relations, gender discrimination and violence, mental health issues, homelessness, sexual abuse, violence, family life, community life, alcohol and drug abuse—all of the experiences caused by settler colonialism and intergenerational post-traumatic stress disorder.

A smaller number of students prefer to discuss economic development and hold as personal models such leaders as Chief Louie of the Osoyoos Indian Band in British Columbia or Governor Bill Anoatubby of the Chickasaw Nation in Oklahoma. Most want to discuss legal issues such as sovereignty, the history of Indian law, and the contemporary reality of Indian people and nations at all levels of the law, in terms of both an overrepresentation in the penal system and in the relationships between the federal government, the states, and the sovereign American Indian nations as well as those between the Canadian government and FNMI people. Indigenous students are also interested in relationships between themselves, their Tribal nations, and the nations of the larger global community, both Indigenous nations and those recognized as nation-states by the United Nations in this hemisphere and the other.

But settler colonialism, imperialism, capitalism, materialism, and development affect and change us all, Indigenous and non-Indigenous alike, through the process of contact and what scholar Rain Prud'homme Cranford calls "friction" in her manuscript in progress, *Gumbo Stories: Quantum Relation-Making Rhetorics in the Creole South.* And with the increasing concern on the part of many regarding our threatened environment and mutual survival that leads to the level of activism we have seen in #IdleNoMore, #NoDAPL, and #MMIW, it should be no surprise that Indigenous students—almost *all* students—want to look at physical health and environmental issues in texts, including our health, Mother Earth's health, and the interrelated health of all the entities with whom we share creation.

PRAXIS

Part One: Story

My teaching has a discernable pattern: Introduction>Exposition> Story>Dialogue, repeating Exposition>Story>Dialogue until making takes place on the students' part. We then wrap up by visiting about what took place that day and tying things together so that at the end of class students both clarify and develop schemata for remembering what they learned.

Story is one of the most persuasive teaching and rhetorical methods. Today this is being recognized beyond Indian Country. But despite an increasing focus on story and storytelling in mainstream spaces, non-Native students still need preparation for such a methodology. Experience has taught me—via comments on teaching evaluations—that one must explicitly and clearly articulate one's pedagogy. I spend time going over this the first day; a small excerpt of my teaching philosophy for class explains:

> An experienced educator of nearly twenty-five years who has worked with diverse populations of students from first grade to the doctoral level, I utilize both Indigenous and Western pedagogical methods. This may be de-centering for those of you who are accustomed to strictly Western educational methods. Because I want you all to be comfortable, I want to explain this a bit here to help us reach our fullest potential in having a productive and enjoyable semester.
>
> Indigenous pedagogies rely heavily on the use of narrative to carry knowledge, often accompanied by the use of other multimodal discourse such as visual narratives in the form of material culture, such as petroglyphs, codices, wampum belts, winter counts, and beadwork, and/or embodied or kinesthetic discourse such as Plains Sign Language or ethos-bearing tattoos. Experiential learning accompanied and complemented narrative and was reinforced by its often-lifelong retellings. Most of all, Indigenous pedagogies are not separated from the rest of what we as Indigenous people see as reality, physical and metaphysical alike. Our ways of learning are embedded throughout our ways of life, and everything, everything that is part of what we see as Life is related and interconnected. We are all related. EVERYTHING is related. This means I am going to tell you stories.

Part Two: Multimodal Contexts

Story is not the only component of Indigenous rhetorics that is used in what I call—after the community designation—"Talking in a Good Way." Both modeling acceptable cultural protocols and studying Indigenous discourse moments are also important. For modeling, I find that fishbowling this technique at the beginning of the semester is helpful. While students are working with partners on an early assignment, I video-record—with their permission—pairs whose interactions are well-balanced and productive when we use Little Bear's Native paradigm as a lens for examining the conversation. In a time when students are increasingly isolated because of our culture's use of technology, I turn the tables by making the technology work for us. Phones and laptops become learning tools in all sorts of ways in my classroom—a subject for another essay. In this moment, however, I am trying to help them learn or relearn interpersonal and group communication skills many of our current students are nearly bereft of. Mainstream culture has hindered their ability to talk, much less talk in a good way, with one another.

For the second part of this effort, studying Indigenous discourse moments, we turn to our course texts. It is helpful to have not only transcribed and collected oratory and early written discourse but also contemporary speeches and other discourse moments involving traditional Indigenous people. Here, it's important to note that when I invoke "tradition," I always define that in my work and to the students as "continuity + change = balance," a nonmathematical equation but one that functions nevertheless, and one that must function for the Tribal nations to maintain both culture and federal recognition. It is also important to provide as much context as possible for the discourse examined. As Craig Womack points out in *Red on Red*, not only is context crucial to cultural integrity when making meaning (51–57), but context also lets us examine the holistic structure of this multimodal discourse and look for common elements, a class activity that directly correlates to my research methodology in *Back to the Blanket* (Wieser).

What we have found in examining social, ceremonial, and diplomatic visiting in traditional contexts provides much that is useful for pedagogy. These settings begin with greetings, which in historical and current ceremonially preparatory discourse acts are typically followed by prayers; tobacco and/or gifts are offered when one comes seeking knowledge and apprenticeship, and pipe-smoking would take place over agreements and in lifting up prayer. In more formal contexts, traditional introductions provide genealogical and autobiographical information about a speaker. And a time and a place are always set for visiting.

Obviously, not all of these activities are appropriate in the context of the classroom. At the beginning of the semester, I actually leave the room for a few minutes until students let me back in, allowing students I have taught in previous semesters to introduce me to new students, and the new students can ask questions about me in any way they want. This demonstrates that in our relationship as teacher and students, we owe each other things. Students also have relationships with one another as members of the course and owe things to each other. They need to understand that maintaining these responsibilities to one another should be reciprocal, and we should always acknowledge these relationships by treating one another with respect. We renew these relationships each time we come together. Greeting one another reinforces this. I take time at the beginning of each class to be human, to talk to students informally as we slowly fill the room. I also set a time and place for visiting, reinforcing the idea that class is a point in time and space set apart from the rest of our lives for us to be together. If we are indeed, as the great N. Scott Momaday's work suggests, humans "made of words" (9), then family is something we speak into being, and, in the best Indigenous practice of making kin where blood relationships don't exist, I make the students in the classes I teach into mine.

After greetings we do the same things people do during other kinds of visits: We recap or review the last time we talked. We remember previous visits. We catch up on what we all have been doing, only in this situation, this mostly consists of what we have been doing for our course outside of class time. Other aspects of social, ceremonial, or diplomatic visiting, such as eating, can happen. In traditional visiting, at a minimum, beverages such as coffee, tea, or water will be served. And again, although there will be prayers in traditional shared meals, the students I teach—hungry, as yours likely are as well—appreciate the food even without the

Figure 1.1. Banaha, a Choctaw dish I have cooked and shared with my students.

prayers (see Figure 1.1).

Though I do not, as one student evaluation claimed appreciatively, "feed . . . students more often than not," I think the value of food in pedagogical practice has been hugely underrated. I almost always eat and drink while researching and preparing for class. I am drinking coffee while writing this right now, and I had a gluten-free muffin and a healthy breakfast bar while writing the previous three paragraphs. If I listed everything I have eaten in the making of this essay, the list would show that producing this piece meant consuming an entire feast. In fact, if we take a further look at visits that involve the making of ideas, alliances, or material culture—visits analogous to classroom contexts like group work, where planning, negotiating, and making take place—we find sharing food to be an even more important part of the multimodal discourse of the traditional setting. When we eat, we commune; we are kin.

CONCLUSION

So many of these traditional practices work into the structure of my classes. And if you are Indigenous yourself or are familiar with Indigenous rhetorical studies and the scholars who make up our community, I imagine you will see these in your own teaching praxis as well. As another teaching evaluation once said, "Dr. W. treats us like human beings." That's a high compliment when understanding those words in the Cheyenne language of my adopted Blackbear relatives. That's the people's word for themselves—*Tsis-tsis-tas.* Human Beings. At the end of the day, that's the best praise for our pedagogical practices we could get.

For those of you for whom this knowledge has been new, in the hopes of sharing that knowledge and spreading this practice

Figure 1.2. At graduation with former students Kingston Pipestem and Basma Mahdi.

further, I offer it now to you as a gift. It never belonged to just me. We can only make the world a better place together.

WORKS CITED

Momaday, N. Scott. *The Man Made of Words: Essays, Stories, Passages.* St. Martin's Press, 1997.

Prud'homme Cranford, Rain. *Gumbo Stories: Quantum Relation-Making Rhetorics in the Creole South.* Unpublished manuscript, 2015.

Silko, Leslie Marmon. *Ceremony*. Penguin, Kindle edition, 2006.

Wieser, Kimberly G. *Back to the Blanket: Recovered Rhetorics and Literacies in American Indian Studies.* U of Oklahoma P, 2017.

Womack, Craig S. *Red on Red: Native American Literary Separatism.* U of Minnesota P, 1999.

Chapter 2

Building Relationships as a Way to Engage in Decolonial Practice

Yavanna M. Brownlee
University of Northern Colorado

THERE IS NO GOOD TIME TO BEGIN TO insert ourselves into a decolonial practice. It is a practice that does not come at us all at once, like an epiphany. Instead, it is more of an accumulation, a snowball of knowledge that has scooped us up and infiltrated the varied levels of our awareness, our interactions, and our practices. We become a speck of dust at the center of a uniquely patterned snowflake that joins in the snowfall, and we join others in learning how to engage in a decolonial practice, part of that blanket of snow that covers the ground that will, as part of the cycle, nurture the earth and those who grow around us. We are part of a collective, a constellation. As a metaphor, this one is not so bad. The journey of a snowflake is long and tumultuous. There can be false starts because snowflakes get tossed around in the atmosphere and not all of them reach the ground. Even then there is no guarantee that an individual snowflake will join others. The journey to understand what decolonization is, what it means to integrate decolonization into a teaching practice, and what it means to be able to practice it intentionally can be much the same as the snowflake. Like all stories, my story of a decolonial classroom practice is incomplete. I am engaging in one moment in a decolonial spectrum, somewhere in between the beginning of the need to engage in decolonial practice and passing into time immemorial. There are varied approaches to starting a decolonial classroom/academic/life practice, and mine is one way of many.

My moment of engaging in decolonial practice started when I came to the study of Indigenous rhetorics through Scott Lyons's "Rhetorical Sovereignty." I brought Indigenous rhetorics to the classroom because of Lyons's call to do so and because so many students know astoundingly little about Indigenous peoples. Many of us start with the goal to share knowledge even if what we know is magnificently dwarfed by the body of knowledge in stories, histories, rhetorics, practices, studies, and lived experiences. What Lyons did was help me to start recognizing the direct impact that colonization has had on me and on many other mixed-blood descendants, along with recognizing the continued impact that colonization has on Indigenous peoples. I made a choice in that moment: if I—a mixed-blood descendant with tenuous and problematic connections to the people I identify with—am the goal of assimilation, then I am going to resist in ways that help others discover reasons to reconnect and/or be allies in resistance.

Diane Million, in "Felt Theory," states that "[t]o 'decolonize' means to understand as fully as possible the forms colonialism takes in our own times" (55). While this statement is not nuanced, because of its removal from context—Indigenous feminisms—it does speak in part to Tuck and Yang's argument in "Decolonization Is Not a Metaphor" that decolonization cannot be detached from Indigenous concerns and contexts, that "[d]ecolonization is accountable to Indigenous sovereignty and futurity" (35). Because decolonization is tied to recognizing the impact that colonization has on people, ways of being, and locations, it is intrinsically tied to Indigenous peoples. Indigenous peoples across the world are negotiating what decolonial practice means for them, as are their allies, and recognizing that decolonization is not just about the past. Decolonization is about recognizing how past colonial actions will shape the future and how Indigenous peoples work to resist colonial actions and to protect their sovereignty now and in the future. As someone who identifies as a mixed-blood descendant, who is an academic educator and scholar, and who holds many other identities, my work is cut out for me. It will continue to be the journey of a lifetime. I have only just started to understand the impact colonization has in my life and the lives of the people I am in relationship with.

My understanding of how settler colonialism affects me started with an interrogation of the racial and gender inequities I observed growing up in western Colorado in the 1980s and 1990s in a predominantly white town where migrant workers were looked down on and where the two same-sex couples I was aware of closeted themselves from most of the town for fear of losing their livelihoods. Since I became more aware of the oppressions and trauma Indigenous peoples have been facing (I was not raised in the community I identify with), my desire to work for change has only grown. Through engaging with the scholarship surrounding decolonial (Cushman, "Face," "Translingual"; Justice; Mignolo; Million; Mohanty; Smith; Sneider; Tuck and Yang), feminist (Ahmed; hooks; Kovach; Mohanty), and queer theories (Morgensen; Smith), along with Indigenous rhetorics and ways of being (Arnold; Banerjee; Cushman, "Face," "Translingual"; Kimmerer; Lyons; Riley Mukavetz; Powell), and through participating in workshops and presentations at conferences, watching webinars, and listening to the stories students have shared with me, I have worked to refine a classroom practice focused on relationship and the whole person that is decolonial in nature. By this I mean that my practice demonstrates a recognition of the influence of settler colonialism in academia through recognizing inequities and working to ameliorate them. Through recognizing students as whole people who have lives outside of the classroom and through recognizing myself in a similar way, I can work to build relationships with students in which I can position myself in a place of support and care rather than as a gatekeeper. These relationships demonstrate my understanding of my responsibilities as an educator and my respect for students and colleagues and how they foster reciprocity through exchanging respect, knowledge, care, and support. They also involve students opening up to and asking for and receiving the support they need to succeed.

Here, to alleviate any confusion, I want to recognize Tuck and Yang's concern about decolonization being just another tag in the list of social justice markers: "Decolonize (a verb) and decolonization (a noun) cannot easily be grafted onto pre-existing discourses/frameworks, even if they are critical, even if they are anti-racist, even if they are justice frameworks. The easy absorption, adoption, and transposing of decolonization is yet another form of settler appropriation" (3). While I do integrate feminist and queer theories and social justice work—especially when recognizing student differences and celebrating them, raising students up, and working to support their needs (in a partial attempt to make up for the inequities in primary and secondary education)—I recognize that this work is also grounded in Indigenous frameworks. Feminist work can trace its roots back to the Haudenosaunee Confederacy (Arnold 35). Many Indigenous practices and relationships, especially as seen in the *Ganoñhéñ·nyoñ*, or the "Thanksgiving Address," are centered on gratitude and respect for peoples, both human and nonhuman. These practices run contrary to Western practices, which are often centered on hierarchy, putting the white heterosexual male at the top of the hierarchy, building down from there, and not recognizing the personhood of nonhuman entities. Instead, everything below the white heterosexual male becomes an entity for use and consumption, a resource. In building a decolonial classroom practice, I work to start with gratitude and respect and to remove as much of the hierarchy as possible, encouraging equity. I do this through building supportive relationships with my students, positioning myself to teach (yes) but also to learn.

As a basic guide to altering classroom practice, I recommend a few changes up front: (1) revise the syllabus so that it is equitable, accessible, and informative; (2) change the grading policy to prioritize effort and engagement over correctness (Inoue has some interesting scholarship on labor-based grading); (3) emphasize student support as needed, regardless of documented need status; (4) revise the texts to, at a minimum, do a better job of representing the student population and, ideally, to forward artists and scholars from marginalized populations (i.e., BIPOC, LGBTQ+, neurodivergent, and differently abled) instead of erasing or tokenizing; and (5) work on representing yourself as a whole person and seeing students as whole people. Consider these steps recommendations that do not have to be done in any particular order. Any one step is a helpful starting place that can work against the settler-colonial narrative that permeates our classrooms by working against the exclusion of students, systemic racism, and demonstrated white privilege embedded in our institutions.

These alterations are decolonial in a number of ways. Recognizing the full personhood of each student—regardless of upbringing, socioeconomic status, quality of education, etc.—leads to recognizing that students have equity; they are entering a class that recognizes that they have a wide range of skills and abilities and that some students need more support. As a group, we can support individual students while working to meet community classroom goals. For example, integrating workdays into the classroom gives students a chance to ask questions and get support from one another and the instructor instead of mining their already busy schedules for time (a resource) to meet with tutoring services or impromptu study groups or attend instructor office hours. Adjusting to a labor-based grading system addresses the effort students put into the class rather than celebrating students who have a better education or a propensity for the class topic. Instructors and peers can support students who have a talent for the tasks and those who need more help so that both can continue to grow and learn. In choosing texts that represent marginalized student populations, instructors can help students see people like them who have succeeded in education, community, social justice, and/or support. They can see how an individual can work to support community-minded goals rather than a hierarchy built on use and indifference. Finally, instructors have to do the same with themselves. They have to see and position themselves in relation to how they are setting up the classroom. Students are not a job; they are a community full of people who are living, thriving, and learning. Instructors serve as elders to share ways of knowing, information, care, responsibility, and life. Part of engaging in this practice as a decolonial process means not just doing the initial work to make change but continuing to engage in the practice, revisiting what works and what doesn't, and working to improve not just the classroom but also the educational environment it exists in.

I started with these same steps, though representing myself and seeing my students as whole people has improved with experience. The real turning point for me was reading Robin Wall Kimmerer's *Braiding Sweetgrass*. The sense of peace and understanding about how relationships work that grew within me as I was reading Kimmerer's text was profound, like coming home to my true self, so much so that I chose to reexamine my teaching practices and how I built relationships with students. The relationships Kimmerer demonstrates between humans and all of our more-than-human relatives are just the type of relationships we should be working on building in our classrooms. Centering Indigenous ways of knowing and doing in my teaching practice is a decolonial move. It became the ground from which I build relationships not just in my classroom practice but also with my colleagues, friends, and family. Centering Indigenous ways of knowing and doing has reshaped *all* of my relationships.

As we start to change classroom practices, we must decide what we want out of our classes—what we want to happen, what we want students to walk away with at the end of the day or at the end of the term, and what we want to make space for. Moving toward a decolonial practice should be part of what we want to happen. This beginning can happen through recognizing the settler-colonial impact of the systems—such as systemic racism, heteropatriarchy, and white privilege—that our students and we participate in and are affected by. Refocusing on centering Indigenous ways of knowing and being, on building equitable, mindful, and responsible relationships, moves us away from settler-colonial systems. This shift is challenging because it steps away from consumer education, in which knowledge is a product for sale and only the best and the brightest succeed. Instead, this shift benefits everyone, allowing everyone to receive the support they need to succeed while also recognizing systemically enforced educational deficits—such as underfunded schools in communities of color and impoverished areas—and individual time constraints and needs, such as meeting family obligations or working. Instructors need to ask a few questions about students so they can better meet student needs. For example, can we take time to understand a student's subjectivity? Maybe the student grew up in or near poverty and is also a student of color. Maybe they are working a job or two along with going to school and are working to support children or parents. These subjectivities also likely affected their primary and secondary education and their home life and constitute only a few of the barriers that the student might face when it comes to learning. Then we need to ask what we can do to support that student and help them succeed. We can easily give them extra time to complete assignments, take time to listen to their stories, and meet with them outside of class—especially during evenings and weekends—to help with composing skills or to review concepts covered in class.

I would argue that making space for building and growing relationships with students is worth doing and that doing so can improve classroom cohesiveness and discussions. Knowing student stories, backgrounds, and needs can assist in shaping the kind of space that would be useful in a classroom, such as space for working on compositions, for having small-group discussions where students might feel more comfortable sharing personal thoughts and ideas, and for having full-class discussions that dig into small details that are productive but tangential to what was originally on the class agenda. In these ways, students can also build beneficial and trusting relationships with one another. With these relationships built and growing, we can start to challenge student conceptions surrounding composition, the purpose and history behind policing, privilege, and so much more. We also need to center Indigenous knowledges, authors, and thinkers so that students not only engage in decolonial classroom practices, but they also learn through the examples of people who have thought about how Indigenous knowledges, lifeways, stories, and futurism can benefit communities grounded in colonial practices, such as academia and the larger Western/Eurocentric social norm. Daniel Heath Justice, in *Why Indigenous Literatures Matter*, highlights what can be done in discussions when students who have built relationships with one another, who are responsible for their words and actions, and who respect each other are challenged and choose to engage:

> Challenge is not the same thing as rejection or dismissal; we can and must have the hard conversations if we have any hope of a better future. We can have sharp, even contentious arguments, but still return to the conversation and to our relationships when we're done; in other words, we can hold each other to account as we hold each other up—they needn't be mutually exclusive practices. We are sorely in need of more accountable kindness in our critical work as well as in our relationships. (xxi)

I have seen these conversations work, seen students share varying perspectives with peers who demonstrate respect through listening and considering the knowledge shared. For example, in an Indigenous literatures course I recently taught, students debated a tough moment in Cherie Dimaline's *The Marrow Thieves*, examining whether Frenchie (the primary character) should have killed Travis (a Native turned Recruiter—i.e., bad guy) after Travis killed a member of Frenchie's created family. The students spent about thirty minutes deciding whether Frenchie should have killed this man and whether he was justified, especially since in the postapocalyptic time of the novel there is no law enforcement. During this same course, we discussed abortion for most of a class period after reading the first section of Louise Erdrich's *Future Home of the Living God*, without anyone becoming visibly upset or getting defensive. A couple of things about this particular class are important to know: (1) most of the students were English education majors and had taken previous classes together, so much of the initial relationship building had already been completed; and (2) I framed the semester by emphasizing equity and respect and made a concerted effort to let everyone who wanted to talk do so. At the end of these discussions, and regularly throughout the semester, I made a priority of expressing my gratitude for their willingness to engage, for their ability to hold respectful discussions, and for their trust in me as their instructor.

These decolonial moves—respect and expressions of gratitude—have worked for me just as well in cultural studies courses and in composition courses as they do in this literature course. The topics change, but students appreciate space to explore concepts. They appreciate the recognition that some topics are difficult to engage with and that they have the right to have feelings about these topics. Students value the recognition of varied perspectives and the trust intrinsic to sharing opinions and experience. They also value the support we can give them when they need help or are not in a place physically or mentally to engage with these topics, especially some of the more difficult topics, such as sexual assault, abuse, eating disorders, or abortion. In the composition classroom, these topics may be less a matter of class discussion but arise more in compositions and research topics, even when discussing literacy and discourse communities. For example, a student recently decided that sexual assault survivors were the discourse community they wanted to discuss. To support this student, who was not comfortable sharing their experience with the class, we met to conference their paper instead of having them participate in workshop, and they met individually with the writing center director for additional feedback. I also let them know that this composition would be difficult to write—but let choosing it be their choice—and made sure they were receiving the mental health support they needed. Students from the same class turned in compositions on internalized homophobia, supporting a trans sibling, and working to counter the rape culture pervasive on our and other campuses. It is not the challenging topics that are really the problem. The problem is the lack of trust and relationships in our classes that holds students back from engaging with these topics.

A relational approach to classroom practice is not a new idea. Relationship building in classrooms helps students to succeed and to know that they matter, as does their lived experience and embodied knowledge. This is not a radical notion. By recognizing that students are people—people who have families, relationships, and jobs; people who carry trauma, learn differently, and engage differently; and, during the recent pandemic especially, people who are experiencing isolation, grief, physical and mental illness, and unknown hardships—just like we are people, we can make space to be flexible, for hard conversations or for silence, to be supportive, to trust, and to build those relationships that are beneficial for all involved. As educators, we are accountable to our students first and foremost. We don't begin to engage in decolonial classroom practices without them to help us find the way. Building relationships with students is one step toward building larger relationships within our institutions to broaden representation, to recognize and celebrate the Indigenous lands we reside on and care for, to help students overcome the barriers to being successful in the ways they choose, and to develop more respectful and equitable classroom practices and institutions.

WORKS CITED

Ahmed, Sara. *Living a Feminist Life*. Duke UP, 2017.

Arnold, Philip P. "'And Now Our Minds Are One': The Thanksgiving Address and Attaining Consensus among the Haudenosaunee." *Native American Rhetoric*, edited by Lawrence W. Gross, U of New Mexico P, 2021, pp. 17–46.

Banerjee, Subhankar, editor. *Arctic Voices: Resistance at the Tipping Point*. Seven Stories Press, 2013.

Cushman, Ellen. "Face, Skins, and the Identity Politics of Rereading Race." *Rhetoric Review*, vol. 24, no. 4, 2005, pp. 389–95. *JSTOR*, www.jstor.org/stable/20176680.

———. "Translingual and Decolonial Approaches to Meaning Making." *College English*, vol. 78, no. 3, 2016, pp. 234–42.

Dimaline, Cherie. *The Marrow Thieves*. Cormorant Books, 2017.

Erdrich, Louise. *Future Home of the Living God*. HarperCollins, 2017.

hooks, bell. *Feminism Is for Everybody: Passionate Politics*. South End Press, 2000.

Inoue, Asao B. *Labor-Based Grading Contracts: Building Equity and Inclusion in the Compassionate Writing Classroom*. WAC Clearinghouse, 2019.

Justice, Daniel Heath. *Why Indigenous Literatures Matter*. Wilfred Laurier UP, 2018.

Kimmerer, Robin Wall. *Braiding Sweetgrass: Indigenous Wisdom, Scientific Knowledge, and the Teaching of Plants*. Milkweed Editions, 2013.

Kovach, Margaret. *Indigenous Methodologies: Characteristics, Conversations, and Contexts*. U of Toronto P, 2009.

Lyons, Scott Richard. "Rhetorical Sovereignty: What Do American Indians Want from Writing?" *College Composition and Communication*, vol. 51, no. 3, 2000, pp. 447–68.

Mignolo, Walter D. "Epistemic Disobedience, Independent Thought and Decolonial Freedom." *Theory, Culture & Society*, vol. 26, no. 7–8, 2009, pp. 159–81.

Million, Diane. "Felt Theory: An Indigenous Feminist Approach to Affect and History." *Native Feminism*, special issue of *Wicazo Sa Review*, vol. 24, no. 2, 2009, pp. 53–76. *JSTOR*, www.jstor.org/stable/40587781.

Mohanty, Chandra Talpade. *Feminism without Borders: Decolonizing Theory, Practicing Solidarity*. Duke UP, 2003.

Morgensen, Scott Lauria. *Spaces between Us: Queer Settler Colonialism and Indigenous Decolonization*. U of Minnesota P, 2011.

Powell, Malea. "Rhetorics of Survivance: How American Indians Use Writing." *College Composition and Communication*, vol. 53, no. 3, 2002, pp. 396–434.

Riley Mukavetz, Andrea M. "Towards a Cultural Rhetorics Methodology: Making Research Matter with Multi-Generational Women from the Little Traverse Bay Band." *Journal of Rhetoric, Professional Communication and Globalization*, vol. 5, no. 1, 2014, pp. 108–25.

Smith, Linda Tuhiwai. *Decolonizing Methodologies: Research and Indigenous Peoples*. 2nd ed., Zed Books, 2012.

Sneider, Leah. "Gender, Literacy, and Sovereignty in Winnemucca's *Life among the Piutes*." *American Indian Quarterly*, vol. 36, no. 3, Summer 2012, pp. 257–87. *JSTOR*, www.jstor.org/stable/10.5250/amerindiquar.36.3.0257.

Tuck, Eve, and K. Wayne Yang. "Decolonization Is Not a Metaphor." *Decolonization: Indigeneity, Education & Society*, vol. 1, no. 1, 2012, pp. 1–40.

Chapter 3

Decolonial Practice as a Path for Community Kindness in the Classroom

Catheryn Jennings
Hamline University

IMAGINE.

It's fall 2020, and it's my first day teaching at a small, metropolitan liberal arts college in the upper Midwest. The class is synchronous online and all first-year, first semester students; today, we are all the new kid. I greet the students, and I make the new kid joke. Honestly, I am digging for cheerful enthusiasm, but with everything going on, it is a challenge. I look out on the sea of black squares (and the two brave souls who actually have their cameras on: one perfectly framed, the other offering just their cheekbones, peering up over the edge of the screen, but at least they are faces). I begin my standard "first day of class" spiel and ask how everyone is doing; I am met with silence. Okay, I ask them what they *need* from this class. A sardonic voice from a black square says, "A fucking break . . . ," and I think, "Okay. I can do that." So this is a story about how I went about giving my students a break by weaving Indigenous understandings of the value and healing capabilities of community, trust, and story with a very Western understanding of vulnerability, creating a space in my first-year writing classroom that offered students a chance to express and shape their voices and to heal, even if only a little, while the world burned around us.

I like to begin all of my classes with questions about students' relationships with writing and what they have been told about college writing. It's always much the same; they're concerned they will be asked to use cold discourse that is free of any individualism and drafted in perfect English grammar. To them, academic writing seems to exist in a vacuum of formality in which their individual knowledges and identities are not welcome. Composition scholar Melanie Kill discusses this initial discomfort of early college writers' struggle with academic genres and identity writing and how their "ability to position themselves deliberately, and thus their self-presentation, is challenged" (216). Likewise, education scholar Julia G. Brooks identifies students' "deep-seated anxiety and/or socialized discomfort with ambiguity that aggravates their already perceived precarious standing in class" (47). In ideal semester circumstances, this journey of expected performance and anxiety while having to navigate their understanding of personal voice is daunting, but what about attempting this when the world is on fire? A seemingly insurmountable task, to be sure.

It was in this navigation between assumptions and anxieties where story became an important tool for my community-oriented classroom. In planning my semester and during the first week of fall 2020, and given the conditions brought on by the COVID-19 pandemic and the limitations of Zoom U, I was working hard to create the best and most welcoming possible space I could for my students. In this space, I was an outsider to the community, just a stranger on a screen, waving my arms around, asking students to share their stories, to open up to me and their peers, to be vulnerable in their narratives—so dang awkward trying to do this online. It was clear early on that we needed to find a common ground to make this class work. By turning to Indigenous pedagogical practices and understandings of community, I was afforded an opportunity for a decolonial intervention of classroom relationality.

In the decade or so I have been teaching first-year writing, my primary goals are always to give students the chance to discover their own voices, to foster a space in which to build a learning community, and to create a story-sharing environment that values vulnerability and willingness to share. In *Indigenous Methodologies: Characteristics, Conversations and Contexts,* Margaret Kovach notes that "[f]or stories to surface, there must be trust" (98). In my experience as both a learner and an educator, the students' assumption of formality in academic writing creates barriers to trust through the fear of failure and a hesitancy to engage in their writing. However, even the most reticent student has a wealth of stories they are generally willing to share, and by giving them a space in which to do so, they bloom.

To create that space, I turned to Indigenous pedagogical theories such as those offered by Lisa King et al., who situate the classroom as a place for "recognizing story as a meaningful, theory-full practice" and who offer a guide for pedagogical practices (9). While this particular classroom space existed only online and in a time that was incredibly difficult, I prioritized designing a course that offered students a meaningful chance to not only explore how they were feeling and to make critical connections through sharing stories, but also to find, grow, and flex their individual authorial voices.

Stories have the ability to teach and to heal; I personally came to understand my place in my own Indigenous community through the stories I was told, and from what I have observed, the telling of stories is a familiar knowledge-sharing and comforting practice for most students. In this particular class, I designed writing assignments that asked students to check in on themselves and their support systems by reflecting on themes such as what they considered "home" and the ways in which they have come to know something as "truth." As a class, we also considered and discussed how and why these myriad connections to home and truth were formed, how they informed the students' "voices," and what that knowledge means to them. As we shared stories and reflected on the ways those stories were formed, students were able to not only model from their peers' stories but also see that there are many ways to come to knowledge and many versions of concepts like "home." Kovach also calls stories "vessels for passing along teaching, medicines, and practices that can assist members of the collective" (95). The goal of these projects was to facilitate a space of care for the self and to build a community of learners working together, along with all the critical inquiry and good writing habits of a writing course. In this space, it was made clear that like writing, it is okay for self-care and growth to need rough drafts and workshopping as we learned together. We also spent class time discussing how to grow from failure and how to navigate the unknown, and I asked for similar reflection during and after each writing project through reflective journaling.

Indigenous pedagogical models have created practices that make intentional space for situating the self and for healing and consideration for the members of the (classroom) community. Louie and colleagues state, “If we can normalize Indigenous methods within the academy, we can begin to dismantle the status quo that uses Western perspectives and methods of education as the default” (23). Kathleen Absolon also reminds us, “We can't dismantle colonized forms of knowledge production using colonial methodologies; we need to both develop a critique and then turn our gaze toward Indigenous tools and knowledge” (97–98). The decolonial concept I worked toward the most that semester was the collective understanding of what our community could look like and the different roles we could all occupy within that community. Creating the space for students to share their stories was only the beginning for our classroom; building a community of learners in which folks felt comfortable sharing their stories was also critical.

Through the journey of learning, knowledge seekers move through many different environments and roles and form many relationships, each adding something to their overall understanding of knowledge. The nature of online learning and social distancing added additional challenges to building our little community; it's hard to make connections to a screen full of boxes and disembodied voices. As a class, we constantly worked on breaking down some of the barriers of the traditional classroom, specifically the “sage on the stage” format of an educator on high, distributing knowledge to the masses, and instead focused on building a community of learning and knowledge sharing through student-led discussions and reflective projects that looked at both successes and failures and the lessons to take from them. There were, of course, challenges. Early conversations were about dealing with challenges at home and school that were significantly affecting their ability to “student” as well as they would have liked. Stories of loneliness and isolation, of stress and fear, dominated our class discussions and my relationships in this community. Shawn Wilson remarks on this when he says, "If Indigenous ways of knowing have to be narrowed through a particular lens, . . . then surely that lens would be relationality" (58). Through this lens, the students in all of my courses and I have a relationship, and that relationship must go both ways.

Relational accountability is a concept inherent to Indigenous understandings of community and knowing (Wilson 82); community and the value of relationships are at the core of the Indigenous worldview, and I and others before me have seen the value of bringing this understanding into the writing classroom. Wilson elaborates on relationship by claiming that Indigenous folks *are* relationships rather than being *in* relationships (80). Karen Redfield sees the potential of Indigenous practices in American writing courses, which are "dynamic sites of contemporary rhetoric" that could deeply benefit from the inclusion of Indigenous storytelling and knowledge-making practices (162). How am I turning to relationality to offer an option for decolonial practices in a writing classroom populated primarily by non-Indigenous folks? Specifically, I use these practices to frame the ways in which I prioritize relationality above all other things in my class.

To prioritize building community, I worked with and made space for the students to offer the support that I would hope a community would offer me. By this I mean that, foremost, I wanted to create an educational space that lifted some of the pressures we were (and still are) experiencing: I eliminated all late penalties, because the students' words do not lose value two weeks after a deadline. Instead of counting off for absence, I reached out to check on students to make sure they were okay, asked how I could help, and offered resources, because sometimes everything is too much and someone reaching out can make all the difference. The students offered me their stories and their knowledges, and in return I was not only respectful of those stories but I also cared about students as individuals and accomplices in our shared journey of learning. But above all, I offered my students compassion and the space to tell their stories as they worked toward the "learning objectives" of the course. The stories students share have value; Redfield asks us to "finally begin to respect the use of this gift [of words] as it has been used by Indian rhetoricians in the continuance of storytelling and the development of rhetorical strategies in English" (162). And King reminds us that we must remember that "[t]he narratives we keep and tell shape our discursive practice, with material consequences" (211). To best create and facilitate a space where students felt comfortable with the vulnerability of writing and sharing stories of self and of home, we spent intentional time reiterating and growing the idea of the classroom as a community built on mutual respect and agency.

In a conversation about Indigenous rhetorical practices, Indigenous scholars and personal mentors Andrea Riley Mukavetz and Malea Powell discuss the practice of asking students to visualize the "web of relations in which their own stories were situated" and "providing a space for students to experience both discomfort and love" (141–42). Discussing and sharing the difficult realities of the first-year college experience during a pandemic, online learning, and the looming outrage and fear following the community violence in our area was challenging and felt vulnerable, so building these relationships was more than just important; it was *necessary* for this classroom space to function and the community to form. As Wilson reminds us, "relationships do not merely shape reality, they are reality" (7). The relationships we built, even if they existed only within the confines of the online classroom (which is certainly not always the case), were the tangible reality of our learning community, which was built through openness and sharing, and those relationships were at the core of the kindness I wanted all of us to practice and the community we were working together to build.

How will the practices of community and story continue to inspire and inform my pedagogical practices? Although I can see how these tools might look like a dismissal of the importance of due dates and attending class, instead I consider the value of student knowledge and the changes in the classroom as a reimagining of the ways student success is measured. Dylan Miner says, "We must be cautious to not focus on what is being made, but rather on the actual process of making and with whom we are doing this work"

(131). By practicing community and turning my concern to the well-being of my students rather than to what they are "making," I found the place where I am learning with and from my students, learning how to apply relational accountability not only to my research but also to my classroom, and facilitating knowledge creation and sharing in a kinder, more communal way.

WORKS CITED

Absolon, Kathleen E. *Kaandossiwin: How We Come to Know*. Fernwood Publishing, 2011.

Brooks, Julia G. "Bearing the Weight: Discomfort as a Necessary Condition for 'Less Violent' and More Equitable Dialogic Learning." *Educational Foundations*, vol. 25, no. 1–2, Winter-Spring 2011, pp. 43–62.

Kill, Melanie. "Acknowledging the Rough Edges of Resistance: Negotiation of Identities for First-Year Composition." *College Composition and Communication*, vol. 58, no. 2, 2006, pp. 213–35. *JSTOR*, http://www.jstor.org/stable/20456935.

King, Lisa. "Rhetorical Sovereignty and Rhetorical Alliance in the Writing Classroom: Using American Indian Texts." *Pedagogy*, vol. 12, no. 2, 2012, pp. 209–33.

King, Lisa, et al., editors. *Survivance, Sovereignty, and Story: Teaching American Indian Rhetorics*. Utah State UP, 2015.

Kovach, Margaret. *Indigenous Methodologies: Characteristics, Conversations, and Contexts*. 2nd ed., U of Toronto P, 2021.

Louie, Dustin William, et al. "Applying Indigenizing Principles of Decolonizing Methodologies in University Classrooms." *Canadian Journal of Higher Education*, vol. 47, no. 3, 2017, pp. 16–33.

Miner, Dylan AT. "Mawadisidiwag Miinawaa Wiidanokiindiwag // They Visit and Work Together." *Makers, Crafters, Educators: Working for Cultural Change*, edited by Elizabeth Garber et al., Routledge, 2018, pp. 131–34.

Redfield, Karen A. "Inside the Circle, outside the Circle: The Continuance of Native American Storytelling and the Development of Rhetorical Strategies in English." *American Indian Rhetorics of Survivance: Word Medicine, Word Magic*, edited by Ernest Stromberg, 2006, pp. 149–64.

Riley Mukavetz, Andrea, and Malea D. Powell. "Making Native Space for Graduate Students: A Story of Collective Indigenous Rhetorical Practice." *Survivance, Sovereignty, and Story: Teaching American Indian Rhetorics*, edited by Lisa King et al., Utah State UP, 2015, pp. 138–59.

Wilson, Shawn. *Research Is Ceremony: Indigenous Research Methods*. Fernwood Publishing, 2008.

Chapter 4

Engaging Native Land and Indigenous Food Sovereignty in a Food Writing Classroom: A Decolonizing Pedagogical Practice

Jaquetta Shade-Johnson
University of Colorado Boulder

A STORY

IN HER POEM "Perhaps the World Ends Here," Muscogee author, musician, and three-time United States Poet Laureate Joy Harjo writes, "The world begins at a kitchen table. No matter what, we must eat to live / The gifts of earth are brought and prepared, set on the table. So it has been since creation, and it will go on." I read this poem aloud on the first day of class to students in my special topics writing studies course on food writing in spring 2020, a semester later disrupted by the COVID-19 pandemic. The students, a mix of undergraduate and graduate students, predominantly journalism majors, predominately white, looked around at one another apprehensively as I read them poetry. Perhaps they expected references to American icons of food culture such as Julia Child or Anthony Bourdain, not a Native poem about a table.

A benefit of this poem for this particular class, though, was that it situated our topic of food in relation to place—a kitchen table—an often recognizable concept that set the students more at ease because of its familiarity. Yet we pushed our discussion of the poem further, to the "gifts of the earth" line, to where our food comes from: the Land, with a capital *L,* in acknowledgment of its sentience (Styles et al. 45–46, 49). From this point, we drew our attention to the fact that we were sitting in a building at a land-grant university built on stolen Native Land (Gould 81; Lee and Ahtone). Land is a foundational topic within American Indian and Indigenous rhetorics (Anderson 161). It quite literally grounds our academic and public discourses of rights, responsibility, and sovereignty. With an awareness that students might or might not have come to this course—or any course—with an orientation toward Indigenous concepts of Land, I attempted to construct this course in a way that fostered an orientation to Indigenous Land-based relationships for students, Indigenous and non-Indigenous alike, and that might enrich this understanding for students who were experienced learners of the Land (Riley Mukavetz and Powell 139). Our classroom community began to build a foundation for understanding the significance of Land in every aspect of writing about food, with the acknowledgment that writing about food inherently means writing about Land, across all cultures and contexts.

Throughout the semester, we returned to the topic of Land many times. Eventually we reached the point that I had been waiting for: our unit on food justice, food security, and food sovereignty. Food insecurity negatively impacts many Indigenous nations, as well as communities of color, stemming from a long history of colonial interference with our food systems, both intentional and incidental, but *always* tied to systemic attempts of conquest, assimilation, and genocide. For Indigenous peoples, food sovereignty is the right to determine our own food systems and is the guiding principle for tribal initiatives to reclaim and restore our ancestral foodways (Segrest; LaDuke; "Food Sovereignty").

We used this class unit to bring together what we'd learned about food writing and Land with the concept of food-related justice as a human right and an initiative for addressing food access and security. We looked at a variety of food maps and read articles from *Gravy*, the Southern Foodways Alliance publication, which is deeply rooted in the connections between food, place, and people. We learned about Steven Alvarez's taco literacy course and about a Black community in the South collaboratively composing a cookbook as a way to share their stories and to address their history of trauma (Arellano; Graff). We visited the sugar camp at our university to experience how real maple syrup goes from tree to bucket to bottle to pancakes. We talked about how this was a foodways tradition stemming back centuries for Native people on Turtle Island and how the practice is connected to the Indigenous food sovereignty movement.

To bring the topic of food sovereignty into the classroom creates opportunities for students to address food justice, food security, and the significance of cultural foods. To learn about food injustice for Indigenous peoples, especially from the viewpoint of an Indigenous person, can empower students to consider food issues in their own communities and to challenge how they think about food and their own food systems. Aside from the critical analysis of food, it also creates opportunities for students to compose narratives of their own foodways and their own concerns. It helps them to better understand their own food systems and the power dynamics therein. After all, "everybody eats," as the expression goes, and everybody has a food story. Beyond that, it prompts students to consider the impact of food insecurity and food justice on communities that may differ from their own, to learn more about the resilience and innovation of communities working to reclaim or rebuild their foodways, and to better understand the power and beauty of that reclamation work.

A CLASSROOM PRACTICE

I offer here a description of a classroom activity from this food writing course, which foregrounds a recipe analysis assignment, followed by a discussion of potential decolonial strategies, options, and possibilities. During a section on recipes and cookbooks, I shared with the class three Indigenous-centric cookbooks for analysis: *Original Local* by Heid E. Erdrich, *The Sioux Chef's Indigenous Kitchen* by Chef Sean Sherman and Beth Dooley, and *The Mitsitam Café Cookbook* from the Smithsonian National Museum of the American Indian by non-Native Chef Richard Hetzler, which I distributed among three small groups. To prompt rhetorical analysis, I asked students questions about their cookbook that can also be applied to *any* cookbook: I asked them to note the basic elements of the cookbook (title, cover art, section headings) before asking them to identify audience, author positionality, temporality, structure, additional features, photography and imagery, and the overarching story of the cookbook.

Afterward, I instructed the groups to select and analyze one recipe from their cookbook, identifying the title of the recipe, any headnotes it included, how it considers the needs of readers, attributions, yield of the recipe, ingredients list, methods/directions, sidebars or text boxes, and whether anyone in the group would ever attempt to make the recipe and why. Initially, students jumped into the analysis labor. Once they moved beyond the basic element questions, however, I began to hear uncertainty arising in their group conversations. After checking in with the groups, they articulated that they were concerned about saying the wrong thing. They were apprehensive about discussing food they were unfamiliar with, beyond the frybread tacos a few of them had tried. The students in that class were conscientious people and wanted to be respectful in their approach. They were invested enough to be careful. I appreciated their conscientiousness, but I let them live in that space of discomfort and of learning for a moment before intervening.

Since each group had a different cookbook and therefore unique topics, I consulted with each group separately. The group analyzing *Original Local* were enthusiastically interested in a Native cookbook from a socioculturally different yet adjacent geographic region. *Original Local* contains not exclusively recipes but also poems and narratives that relate to Erdrich's recipes. As Erdrich draws many of the recipes from her family and Tribal community of the Turtle Mountain Ojibwe band, the cookbook centers on food practices of the Anishinaabeg. The students in that group acknowledged never having seen "drawings" or illustrations in a cookbook before, nor resources for purchasing, growing, or foraging the necessary ingredients (Erdrich 17). They had never seen an ingredients list that asked anything more of them than a trip to the supermarket. They were surprised that the cookbook asked readers to forage dandelion greens or to use wild game, if they had access to it. If not, "store bought is fine," to borrow a catchphrase from celebrity chef Ina Garten of *The Barefoot Contessa.* Erdrich helpfully suggests appropriate substitutions for difficult-to-find ingredients, as well.

The group of students who analyzed Chef Sean Sherman's award-winning *The Sioux Chef's Indigenous Kitchen* were, at first glance, confronted with what seemed like a standard American cookbook, with a familiar layout and more recipes and guides than supplemental narrative. The recipes came from the upper Great Plains region of Minnesota and the Dakotas. As the students read more closely, they began to point out the unique ingredients. Sherman's book, like Erdrich's, instructs readers to utilize game and wild foods, if they have access. Like *Original Local,* Sherman's cookbook features locally sourced, seasonal dishes. The students analyzing this text were surprised to find the section headers listed in the table of contents not as Appetizers, Entrées, Desserts, etc., as conventional cookbooks tend to do, but instead were categorized by Fields and Gardens, Prairies and Lakes, and Nature's Sweets, Teas, and Refreshing Drinks. They were excited to see that cookbooks can be organized in a variety of ways, that they do not have to follow a conventional structure—that cookbooks, or any food writing, do not have to function within the confines of hegemonic food writing standards.

The group who read *The Mitsitam Café Cookbook* (Hetzler) discovered a conventional cookbook structure that guided their way, though they found it challenging to identify a comprehensive overarching story from the text, which features the pan-Indigenous cuisine served at the café of the Smithsonian National Museum of the American Indian. Their experience with this text, however, created an opportunity to compare it with the two Native-authored Indigenous cookbooks analyzed and presented by their classmates. This facilitated questions such as "What does it look like when Native people are the authors of their own cookbooks and recipes?" and "What if this cookbook isn't written for you?" These questions were new concepts for most of the students, many of whom had never before challenged, through such a local lens, the access that comes with settler colonialism, nor its imposed and assumed ownership of stories and systems outside of its own—especially not while reading cookbooks. The students rose to this challenge in their group discussions, however, and opened themselves up to a different way of thinking about the power systems that benefited many of them. I was surprised at their investment as they thoughtfully and carefully responded to these questions in small- and large-group conversations, collectively pulling at the loose threads of Manifest Destiny and settler ideology as they worked through discussions about Indigenous representation in (food) writing and Indigenous people's ownership of and access to their own (food) stories.

Beyond that, however, this activity led us to fruitful conversations about how integral Land is to Native food practices, how the foods we cook are rhetorical productions of the Land, how these rhetorical productions are tied intrinsically to Land-based relationships, how our histories shape these relationships, how our foodways are disrupted by settler colonialism, and how Native peoples continue to do the work of reclaiming and maintaining those relationships with the Land.

A DISCUSSION

The activity described in this chapter is one example of my pedagogical practices. Yes, the texts I distributed to the group were Native cookbooks, but the activity could easily be adapted for a variety of cookbooks and recipes from any cultural community, as well as by any instructors working to disrupt colonial and/or Western codes of food writing. The design of this activity offers students the concept of "options," a significant factor of decolonial pedagogy (Mignolo and Walsh 83, 86, 212). It makes visible to them the idea that writing (in their case, food writing) does not have to be modeled after the conventions they have seen before, that they can move beyond the binary of correct and incorrect, that other models are possible.

Further, this activity helps students to understand the rhetoricity of Land and rhetorical productions of the Land, including foodways and materiality. It offers opportunities for learning to subvert the pervasive Romantic mythos associated with Indigenous peoples and our ties to the Land. This in turn initiates the opportunity for students to learn more about the historical and continual impact of Land policy on Indigenous communities and nations, and to begin recognizing the rhetorics of settler colonialism as a systemic, Land-commodifying form of oppression. By emphasizing a decolonial framework for considering Indigenous relationships with Land, students benefit from critical inquiry into rhetorical histories and current realities of the (food) cultures and (food) systems within which they participate. We address topics ranging from settler narratives of Manifest Destiny to the Columbian Exchange and the slave trade, to forced removals, relocations, and Land allotment to access to cultural foods and materials, to borders, borderlands, immigration policies, and migrant labor to water scarcity, to climate change and the impact of all of these issues on our food, our bodies, our environments, our cultures, and our communities. In a class such as this one, my intention is to build space and possibility for students to strengthen their understanding of the reciprocal relationships of Indigenous peoples, our foodways, and the Land as a pathway to reducing settler harm, and to empower them to address the injustices within their own unique cultural systems—food or otherwise.

At the end of the 2020 spring semester, students in my food writing course were given the option to write either a food memoir narrative or a course reflection essay as their final project. By then the COVID-19 pandemic had begun to take its devastating toll on humanity on a global scale and necessitated a shift at my university, as for many others, from in-person class to online instruction. The students and I had not seen each other in the physical classroom for nearly two months at that point and were so far removed from the dynamic of the first week of class and our early Indigenous cookbook analysis activity that I did not expect the students to focus on Indigenous food sovereignty and food justice as their takeaways from the course. But each of the students who chose to write reflections of their class experiences referred directly to the impact of those specific lessons and concepts. One student reflected, for example, that she was leaving the course with the understanding that "food writing can also be about class and cultur[al] commentary, about social justice issues, and about our relationship to the earth." This understanding is the most for which I could have hoped—for students whose lives had been abruptly and indefinitely uprooted during a worldwide public health crisis to acknowledge these teachings and to carry them beyond the class.

WORKS CITED

Anderson, Joyce Rain. "Remapping Colonial Territories: Bringing Local Native Knowledge into the Classroom." *Survivance, Sovereignty, and Story: Teaching American Indian Rhetorics,* edited by Lisa King et al., Utah State UP, 2015, pp. 160–69.

Arellano, Gustavo. "Are You Taco Literate? Lessons from Steven Alvarez." *Gravy.* Southern Foodways Alliance, Winter 2016, www.southernfoodways.org/are-you-taco-literate/. Accessed 28 Mar. 2017.

Erdrich, Heid E. *Original Local: Indigenous Foods, Stories, and Recipes from the Upper Midwest.* Minnesota Historical Society Press, 2013.

"Food Sovereignty." *Honor the Earth.* Honorearth.org. Accessed 9 Oct. 2020.

Gould, Janice. "The Problem of Being Indian: One Mixed-Blood's Dilemma." *De/Colonizing the Subject: The Politics of Gender in Women's Autobiography,* edited by Sedonie Smith and Julia Watson, U of Minnesota P, 1992, p. 81.

Graff, Michael. "Recipes in Black and White. *Gravy.* Southern Foodways Alliance, 31 July 2020, www.southernfoodways.org/recipes-in-black-and-white/.

Gravy. Southern Foodways Alliance, www.southernfoodways.org/gravy/. Accessed 31 July 2020.

Harjo, Joy. "Perhaps the World Ends Here." *The Woman Who Fell from the Sky.* W.W. Norton, 1994, p. 68.

Hetzler, Richard. *The Mitsitam Cafe Cookbook: Recipes from the Smithsonian National Museum of the American Indian.* Fulcrum Publishing, 2010.

LaDuke, Winona. "Seeds of Our Ancestors, Seeds of Life." *TEDxTC. YouTube,* 4 Mar. 2012. Accessed 12 June 2020.

Lee, Robert, and Tristan Ahtone. "Land-Grab Universities: Expropriated Indigenous Land Is the Foundation of the Land-Grant University System." *High Country News,* 30 Mar. 2020, www.hcn.org/issues/52.4/indigenous-affairs-education-land-grab-universities.

Mignolo, Walter D, and Catherine E. Walsh. *On Decoloniality: Concepts, Analytics, Praxis*. Duke UP, 2018, pp. 83–212.

Riley Mukavetz, Andrea, and Malea D. Powell. "Making Native Space for Graduate Students: A Story of Collective Indigenous Rhetorical Practice." *Survivance, Sovereignty, and Story: Teaching American Indian Rhetorics,* edited by Lisa King et al., Utah State UP, 2015, pp. 138–59.

Segrest, Valeria. "Food Sovereignty." *TEDxRainier. YouTube,* 23 Jan. 2014. Accessed 12 June 2020.

Sherman, Sean, with Beth Dooley. *The Sioux Chef's Indigenous Kitchen.* U of Minnesota P, 2017.

Styres, Sandra, et al. "Toward a Pedagogy of Land: The Urban Context." *Canadian Journal of Education*, vol. 36, no. 2, 2013, pp. 34–67, https://journals.sfu.ca/cje/index.php/cje-rce/article/view/1293.

Chapter 5

Tending the Fire: Graduate Mentoring as Decolonial Practice

Cindy Tekobbe
University of Illinois Chicago

THE METAPHOR OF FIRE HISTORICALLY stands in for everything from passion to creation to change to eternity. For Native Americans, fire is used in ceremony for its inspiration, its transformative nature, and its purifying smoke in ceremony. In this chapter, I invoke the metaphor of fire as the transformative potential of graduate student experiences. I write to describe my Indigenous mentoring practices and how I see them as supporting and sustaining the creative, transformative, and sacred community of graduate students. While approaches to student mentoring are always an important discussion, I am writing this chapter in the summer of 2021 while the COVID variants continue to spread, threatening the health and safety of our campus community. COVID, low pay, substandard health care, visible disability, and white supremacy are identifiable challenges for graduate students. The invisible is harder to see, such as student mental health struggles, certain disabilities, and personal and interpersonal struggles that are typically viewed as beyond our scope as mentors. Here in the Deep South, on our campus at the University of Alabama where I teach and research, there is a darker history of white supremacy, including buildings built by the enslaved, buildings named for prominent segregationists, and significant moments in the Civil Rights Movement of the 1950s and 1960s. This complex history and significant backdrop to the Bama experience further nuances the challenges faced by my graduate students, who must negotiate this history and context into their own understanding of the institution and of research and learning, and it elevates the urgency of tending the sacred fire in them.

I construct this piece in conversation with the rich history of mentoring scholarship in our field. Many of these texts helped shape my thinking around mentoring relationships and responsibilities, such as Michelle F. Eble and Lynée Lewis Gallet's 2008 edited collection, *Stories of Mentoring: Theory and Praxis* and Ana Milena Ribero and Sonia C. Arellano's 2019 *Peitho* article, "Advocating Comadrismo: A Feminist Mentoring Approach for Latinas in Rhetoric and Composition." I read Ribero and Arellano's concept of *comadrismo* with joy for its Latina rhetorics that situate female mentoring relationships rooted in intersectional feminism and inclusivity. As an Indigenous auntie, I come to graduate mentoring with a decolonial framework of disrupting the Western subordinate relationship between mentor and mentee. A decolonizing mentoring framework features working with good hearts for the good of each other, working in good and right relations for generosity with each other, working in good intentions by being honest and sincere with each other about our objectives, and undermining settler ideology, knowledge practices, and colonizing strategies. Within my Indigenous framework, students are colleagues, working in community with me, and when I stoke this community fire, I enable and support student agency. These relationships help make visible the invisible challenges students face. These things can be hard to come by in the top-down Western traditions of teaching and learning. I am applying these decolonial methodologies as I think through my own mentoring story, and I invite you to join me in this collaborative thinking.

When I locate myself for audiences, I say I am a Native feminist and I am Choctaw, Irish, and English. I have never had strong ties to the Irish and English branches of my family. Rather, I grew up in an extended family network of Choctaw uncles, aunties, and cousins. We cooked together, ate together, and lived in one another's orbits. My late aunt and mother wrangled us, gave advice, and maintained family history and culture. They held us together (a role my sister and cousin hold now) through adversity and loss. And together we all maintained the metaphorical fire of the sacred—of family and community. I struggled a bit when I began my graduate studies because balancing my family life with my education was sometimes difficult. Additionally, I am no one's elder—a traditional knowledge keeper who is typically of the older generations—and because of this, the scholarly act of positioning myself as a knowledge maker and keeper was something I was constantly negotiating for myself. Finally, I worried about publishing because what I say and do is always in good relations with my family who, like many Native folx, do not value or trust settler institutions, and I don't want to stray too far from the inherent trust in our familial relationships. There is a history and a context of institutionalization and colonization in public education for Indigenous peoples that I must navigate while staying true to my Indigeneity. It is a long history of genocide—of kidnapped children and holding them hostage to ensure adult compliance, of boarding schools, of enforced missionary conversation, of forced labor, and of physical and sexual abuse. It is a story that underpins all my interactions with settler educational institutions. As a Native academic, I negotiate this history every day and in every interaction with the institution and its agents.

These are not uncommon struggles for Indigenous students. I have mentored Indigenous undergraduates, and their concerns included desiring a sense of community, carrying a belief that they would not be understood, and longing for cultural immersion. They wanted their learning embedded in their cultures and communities. Mentoring in undergraduate Native culture, primarily Diné culture, during my doctoral work at Arizona State University was a matter of negotiating the colonial issues I describe while elevating Diné lifeways, such as close attention to spirituality and ceremony and careful attention to student privacy. These were practices I was familiar with. Now that I am an assistant professor, mentoring graduate students at a primarily white institution (PWI) is more of a struggle because I must begin with offering decolonial perspectives on how they think about scholarship and professionalism. I must begin by introducing them to my context and my "why" before I start on my "how." I explain this here with an example from my own story of being a Native graduate student in a primarily white program.

When I was a doctoral student, I received the conventional wisdom and advice that I should work solely on my own scholarship without collaboration because we are only our own work in academe. In decision-making, I was advised that I should do what was best for myself alone because, of course, I was the sole beneficiary of my work. While well-meaning and genuinely caring, this advice was in direct conflict with my Indigenous lifeways. I do not want to do what is best for me but what is best for my relations network—my community—and what will be acceptable and best for my relations and elders, my family. This includes me but is not only me. I am motivated and identified through my relations, not in isolation from them. And in fact, doing what is best for oneself is the crux of a colonial, capitalist culture, one that is based on and celebrates personal achievement and discounts collaborators and cultural support systems—and one that suggests that personal achievement is the only meaningful, satisfying, and, most important, desirable outcome, even at the expense of others. But I am not only myself; I am also my Indigenous family and my greater community. And my accomplishments are made meaningful within the context of my collective kinship network and network of relations. I make them proud. These were my earliest Indigenous cultural lessons, that meaning is made through good relations, openness, with good intent, and within community and relationships.

I am not arguing here that mentoring students with Indigenous cultural and social practices can solve the larger structural problems of the precarity of graduate students. Or that this mentoring can magically erase the invisible and visible obstacles to good mental and physical health that graduate students face. I do think Indigenous mentoring can be a countervoice to that colonial-capitalist narrative of individualism that isolates graduate students emotionally and professionally, and the narrative that requires graduate students to put on a performance of individual perfection rather than present as their authentic selves. As an Indigenous mentor largely mentoring white students at a PWI, I designed my graduate mentoring processes around meaning-making and meaningful making with my colleagues-mentees. I grounded my practices in the Indigenous notion of good relations, one that positions participants as relatives and greets them with a mind open to collaboration and support.

From the starting point of good relations, I developed three basic categories of mentoring activities. The first is checking-in, as a way to form relations and relationships. The second is storytelling, as a way to honor each other, affirm our labors, engage each other ethically, and solve problems. The third is celebration and ceremony, as a way to mark the passing of time and development of the student—to notice, draw attention to, and value the day-to-day achievements that build on one another and lead eventually to the thesis or dissertation defense.

I think about checking in as first, connecting, and as second, refreshing the connection. I want my students to know not only that I have thought about them but also that I continue thinking about them. That *they* are important, not just their work, and that they and their work matter to me. So I check in at least once every three weeks, about five times a semester, depending on whether I can interact with them at program events. During this pandemic, I have been reaching out a bit more since we do not have in-person programming right now. Knowing that an unexpected email from an advisor can be anxiety-inducing, I am careful to check in regularly instead of just when things are due or workshops are scheduled. An email with one or two sentences noting that I am checking in and asking how they are doing and if they need anything, sentences that reinforce what I ask them when I see them in person, is usually safe enough. I read through their answers and—this is important—accept their words at face value because the point of the practice is to let them know I am thinking of them, not to create any obligation for them to tell me anything. It is the practice of decolonial kinship in which I respect their rights to their own stories and their choice of whether to tell those stories.

This morning I emailed a mentee whom I had not seen in the hall. We typically pass by each other during a class changeover, but not on that day. The email I sent was brief, asking how they were and reminding them that I was available to read those draft pages they asked about the last time I saw them. They wrote back, and we had a brief but friendly conversation about their classes and their friends in the cohort they had seen recently. I have certainly had deeper conversations with them in person, but this email was about renewing the lines of communication and reminding them that we have this collaborative and collegial relationship. In addition to my regular office hours, I try to hold weekly open office hours at the local coffee shop or on Zoom. For example, when I go to the coffee shop to write, I send an email letting my students know that I am writing, where I will be, and that they are welcome to join me. I remember being a graduate student when my mentor invited me to write with her and how much it meant to me to have someone to sit with instead of working on my own. When I have a few solid hours of grading to do, I leave my Zoom up and open with my personal link (which is always posted to my course Blackboards), and that little ding lets me know when a grad student stops in.

Initially in the semester, students will just use the open Zoom time to ask questions, but later in the semester, when our relationships are stronger, they will also just drop in to say hi. This strategy works well with undergraduates too, who often pop in just to say hello. Sometimes students will tell me stories about their week or their families, and I listen in community with them, supporting and encouraging their prioritization of their health and family time. I am also transparent about my work and my own challenges. I told them when my mother's life was ending and I was traveling to be with her during a time of heavy COVID restrictions. I told them when I was feeling challenged by my own monograph. I told them why I was leaving class early when my nephew had been hospitalized and my sister needed support. While I believe there are many things that are too personal to share outside the limited configuration of family network, I also believe that prioritizing my own health and family in a visible way can demonstrate to my students a non-Western way to be an academic.

Today I checked in on a doctoral student who has finished coursework and is beginning to prepare for their exams. We exchanged emails and they told me they were struggling a bit with momentum in writing their prospectus. I remember those days when coursework and exams were over and all I had to do was put down on paper what my project was and how I was going to accomplish it. In other words, I was hung up on what is probably the most difficult step in the path to candidacy, and this student was as well. They told me a little about what was going on, although they could not really explain why their progress was stalling. I read carefully and asked a few questions. I told them this situation was not uncommon. Then I shared with them the story about how I got really bogged down at this point in my journey. I was up to my eyeballs in angst and self-doubt. Finally, I talked to Professor Shirley Rose, who was a member of my dissertation committee. She listened, told me my struggle was common, and gave me a few pointers on how to get unstuck. For example, prioritize my writing, schedule time for my writing, really think through the order of my priorities, and set smaller goals. This advice really helped me out, but the human connection with my professor helped me more.

I told this story to my student, the story of what it took to overcome being intimidated by my scholarly elders and approach them for help. The important thing, I told my student, was to be gentler with the self. I shared stories of my own isolation and impostor syndrome. I listened closely and carefully to my student's stories, and I affirmed and normalized vulnerability and self-doubt. Self-recrimination for not being "good enough" or "far along enough" is energy that is not going into positive things; this is not tending the fire. And I continued to listen while offering affection, kinship, and affirmation of their work beyond a perceived settler time when everything must be accomplished the same way, with that same grueling process, because settler morality centers the uniformity of the product and the conformity of production. Decolonial time is in the process and the lifeway. It is about knowing when your productivity for the task is over and knowing when you are inspired. And if you lack inspiration, return to the things you value about the task. Warm yourself by the fire.

The last item on my mentoring list is to celebrate day-to-day successes. I remind students that research and writing are ceremony, and those seemingly small gains are important and mark progress, success, and self-growth. Here I want to say that perhaps for some people, moving through the daily demands of graduate school without regular affirmation or celebration of those small accomplishments is a simple matter of doing the tasks, checking the boxes, and believing in themselves. A simple task of embracing the settler individualism narrative. For me, it was not simple. I was used to a persistent engagement with my community-family. I needed that level of connection, of affirmation, and graduate school is not designed to provide that. And how I create and make and do does not align well with checking boxes and doing rote tasks. This affirmation, then, is something I provide to my students through mentoring. I try to help them see beyond models of capitalist production, of assembly lines, and of rigid efficiency. I try to engender creative imagination as a way of writing and doing. Imagine existing in a space where there are no arbitrary constraints pulled from a workplace that promotes hierarchy of ability and meritocracy that benefits the status quo. In this space, theorizing and synthesizing an approach to something new is not impossible. It is instead a creative act. And we are collaborators and creators, and that is worth celebrating.

I am not saying that you can do anything you set your mind to, because that is an ableist and neoliberal bootstrap narrative that places community responsibilities onto the individual and then blames the individual for the inability to be a community on their own. A settler-colonial system tells us how to be a gender, a class, a race, a sex, an identity, and those settled boundaries are unmovable. Graduate students are currently doing transformative work within a settler context that does not allow for transformation. Therefore, graduate students face all manner of personal, cultural, intellectual, and social barriers. But graduate work is about the possibility of transformation and the creation of new knowledge, so we must decolonize the mentoring process and open and hold space for the possibilities of inclusive kinship. Transgressing these barriers and expectations can be celebrated as simply as offering a smile and a show of support, something like, "You were great!" Or "I really enjoyed reading the latest iteration of your argument." Or even just making a little time to talk in the hallway. Affirmation comes in many forms, and it is free. Academia is not a zero-sum game, and we can build up that fire as often as we are able.

I began this piece with the metaphor of tending a fire. Tending a fire is a different thing from starting a fire. Tending a fire requires a nuanced understanding of how a fire works. It needs kindling to spread, it needs oxygen to grow, and it needs fuel to persist. Tending a fire is a knowledge practice that is contemplative, attentive, and progressive. Keeping a fire alive is ceremony and medicine. Ceremony is the ritual and mindful practices that celebrate the individual components that make fire, and medicine is the fire sharing its warmth and light with us. I think new graduate students arrive with the fire already burning, in that they worked hard to get to graduate school and they are inspired by learning from other scholars and the possibilities of new knowledge creation. We just need to tend that fire by centralizing decolonial practices in graduate programs that are collaborative, communal, and celebratory.

WORKS CITED

Eble, Michelle F., and Lynée Lewis Gaillet. *Stories of Mentoring: Theory and Praxis*. Parlor Press, 2008.

Ribero, Ana Milena, and Sonia C. Arellano. "Advocating Comadrismo: A Feminist Mentoring Approach for Latinas in Rhetoric and Composition." *Peitho*, vol. 21, no. 2, Spring 2019, pp. 334–56, https://cfshrc.org/article/advocating-comadrismo-a-feminist-mentoring-approach-for-latinas-in-rhetoric-and-composition/.

Chapter 6

A Writing Center's Place Is in the #Community: Decolonizing Writing Center Administration

Deidre Anne Evans Garriott
University of South Carolina

AT FACE VALUE, WRITING CENTER pedagogies may seem more inclusive than some others in traditional writing studies, and they have been moving toward increasingly progressive positions within the last few years. Even so, writing center professionals are urging one another to move beyond calls for change; we are demanding real changes in our scholarship, pedagogies, practices, and professional organizations. Writing center administrators (WCAs) have documented that BIPOC students and tutors are aware of the social and racial injustices in writing centers. In reflecting on her experiences as a graduate tutor at a predominantly white institution (PWI), Anna Treviño asserts,

> Rhetorical spaces can welcome a person's certain culture and identity while also rejecting a person's other culture(s) and identities—the denial of the possibility of the Third Space and the severing of the Third Space into only two possibilities. The rhetorical spaces of PWIs are spaces of such violence for students who are not white, middle-class men because it is their cultures, identities, and even phenotypes that are embedded en los ladrillos y el cemento. (Faison and Treviño)

Treviño's story and analysis are helpful when we remember that writing centers are often staffed by a largely homogenous, primarily white cohort, especially those drawing from English departments.

The dominance of whiteness is not accidental; the traditional university system in the United States is built on Euro-American rhetorical practices, including logical structures and embodiment. Therefore, writing centers are part of the colonization, especially considering the ways that centers have, historically, produced language homogeneity. To decolonize any space is to consider the bodies there—the people in it, their histories, and their many languages—and then consider how the university (the space) has oppressed their bodies, histories, and languages under the pretense of taming them (i.e., making them white in practice) (Powell 401). But WCAs must move past consideration, which is the bare minimum of allyship and where most white scholars seem comfortable. It is imperative that white WCAs confront our complicity in the colonial system.

The university where I instruct writing courses and direct the Writing Center, the University of South Carolina (USC), has a nearly invisible Indigenous population, even though the campus is built on Cherokee and Catawba land. As of writing this chapter, the Office of Multicultural Student Affairs' website neither mentions nor offers resources for Indigenous students, faculty, or staff. According to USC's 2024–25 demographic report, Indigenous students represent such a fractional percentage of the student population that they are not represented on the pie chart (University of South Carolina). It should come as no surprise, then, that the Writing Center's tutoring staff is predominantly white and has not represented the Indigenous people (federally recognized or not)[1] on campus or in the state. My university and my writing center are not doing enough toward decolonization, and while there are constraints that make this work difficult, they do not make it impossible.

As a white, cis woman in a majority-white space, it feels disingenuous to offer advice about decolonizing writing centers when Indigenous voices and people are not present. But as someone mentored by Indigenous women, I have tried to take a decolonial orientation to tutor education specifically, as well as in my collaborations with other academic units. In fact, as I have written and revised this chapter, I have questioned (and continue to) what I can contribute to this project. But what I can do is demonstrate how writing center administrators can position their centers and prepare their staff to tackle the writing center's historical role in colonization vis-à-vis academia. In this chapter, I offer what decolonial work might look like for WCAs in order to provide a sense of possibility, a possible direction, to help us move closer toward joining the decolonial project. Moreover, I define decoloniality in writing centers as making visible and legible the needs and practices of local Tribal nations and working toward ending the dominance of whiteness (of thought, of staffing, etc.) in our centers and on our campuses.

STAFFING

It is impossible to generalize the power of WCAs to make staffing decisions. For example, I do not make any staffing choices; instead, tutors for my center come from the Department of English's first-year MFA and MA cohorts, and because I am nontenure track and not on the admission committee, I do not influence decisions about new students. Some WCAs have agency to make all of their staffing decisions. However, when WCAs cannot (or do not) control staffing decisions or choose to hire staff who reflect a white WCA's experiences, the staff suffers. More egregiously, the dominance of white tutoring staff enacts violence on BIPOC students when tutors uncritically tutor students to translate their dialects into academic standard English (Young 50). Faison and Treviño, Jackie Grustch McKinney, and others have shared stories about the experiences BIPOC tutors have had in writing centers, especially to challenge the myths of what McKinney calls "grand narratives" about writing centers, and particularly their "safe" reputations. Colonialism has made writing centers unsafe for anyone who is not white and middle class.

Tutors themselves may suffer from the violence of whiteness. Tutors are not exempt from feeling excluded. Wonderful Faison shares that while she was a tutor at a writing center at a PWI, her fellow tutors called into question her knowledge and expertise, especially when she tutored Black clients, and white clients assumed she was the receptionist (Faison and Treviño). As Faison and Treviño point out, colonialism's effects extend into how (un)comfortable BIPOC tutor experience work can be in the writing center.

Equally related to staffing are the ways that clients and tutors see themselves reflected in the demographics of the profession. When writing centers are staffed by primarily white tutors, the centers' governing units and indeed their institutions send a message about who is in positions of authority. And yes, tutors, even peer tutors, are in positions that clients will perceive as authoritative. When BIPOC clients come to a center staffed primarily by white tutors, they do not see themselves reflected in the staff. They do not see their experiences, culture, knowledge, habitus, and methods. They see instead yet another place in the academy that will erase everything that has informed them to date and require them to replace those things with Western practices.

My fellow WCAs and I know the problems we face with staffing, but I am challenging us to draw attention to the ways in which accepting staffing procedures as permanent barriers perpetuates colonization. So what can we do? We must make visible the problems that our staffing models create, and that visibility must be clear in both our direct reports (in my case, to my department chair) and to ourselves. Namely, we must push to make Tribal nations and Indigenous students part of our centers, but we must do so in ways that do not tokenize Indigenous students. To do this, we must change our recruiting practices and rethink the qualities that we assume make an applicant a "good" tutor.

So what might this look like? I am not entirely sure myself even as I am fighting this battle—but maybe the fight itself is a part of the decolonizing journey. Some ways that I am reflecting on the challenges of this fight include critical reflection and focusing on relationships. We can make contact with the Tribal leaders in our communities to learn about writing and writing needs in their communities. There is more to learn about writing and writers by setting aside Euro-American ways of knowing and instead listening to the Indigenous leaders in our local areas. I am interested in further understanding how to carry what we learn back into our centers and to share with our campus leaders who affect our staffing decisions. We need to push for increased university recruitment of and funding for Indigenous students so that we are affecting the entire campus, not just our centers and therefore ourselves.

TUTOR EDUCATION

WCAs are largely drawing from feminist and student-centered practices in tutor training. Our professional organizations have promoted antiracist theories and practices, better access for students with disabilities, and improved practices of inclusion. But most of us, as a field, have neglected decoloniality in tutor training and our own continuing educational paths. In this section, I suggest that WCAs think about nonlanguage ways of learning and knowing. I have benefited by drawing from cultural rhetorics scholarship, especially the intersections of visual, material, and embodied ways of learning, rather than leaning on what is traditional—or rather, Euro-American.

For example, I have moved toward visual ways of understanding academic narratives to promote writing as a form of storytelling, a concept I have drawn from the Cultural Rhetorics Theory Lab's "Our Story Begins Here: Constellating Cultural Rhetorics" (Powell et al.). Each year the tutors and I study logical structures of other cultures so that rather than "correcting" the Writing Center's structure and organization to reflect Euro-American, linear structures, we come to understand and promote different structures. From past lessons, I have learned that many of our students do not have formal training in logical structures. This next academic year, I will have the tutors literally draw what logic means to them. Pulling from material rhetorics theory and Marilee Brooks-Gillies's scholarship on crafting and rhetoric ("Constellations"; *Crafting Place*), I have developed an inquiry-based experience centered on crafting that focuses on the role of embodiment to inform makers about the interconnectedness of teaching and learning. The goal of crafting in Writing Center training is to emphasize sharing, making, and community/coalition building as learning rather than hoarding knowledge and skills through nondirective tutoring practices that the writing center community has long celebrated. In sum, these are the questions I'm pursuing:

- What are ways that we can think more locally about where we are, what we do, and how we know what we are doing?
- How can we apply principles of decolonization to fight the privatization of learning, the way traditional higher education treats knowledge as hidden and passed from one authority to select students?
- How can we create a community in which participants learn from and teach one another?

BUILDING COMMUNITIES OF RESISTANCE ON AND OFF CAMPUS

Thus far, I have described a constellated approach to building a community that avoids as much as possible the continuing colonization innate within the US academic project. The community of learning should not stop within our centers; we should take time to teach and learn from our campus partners—and from our local communities. Achille Joseph Mbembe argues, "[W]hen we say access, we are not simply thinking in demographic terms, although these are crucial. When we say access, we are also saying the possibility to inhabit a space to the extent that one can say, 'This is my home. I am not a foreigner. I belong here.' This is not hospitality. It is not charity" (30). While Mbembe speaks of buildings, specifically of removing the iconography of colonizers from his South African campus, his demand that higher education campuses feel like home—are home—to their communities is critical to my imagining of building communities.

I offer two ways that we can imagine possibilities for writing center professionals to take part in decolonial writing centers through community building. I have argued for the importance of the visibility of Indigenous practices in the writing center; here, I extend that argument to insist that WCAs interested in resisting colonization vis-à-vis higher education must actively dismantle the systems that oppress and erase our Indigenous communities. That dismantling is critical to creating a home by resisting the concept that higher education is a charitable structure.

First, WCAs should hold up a mirror to our colleagues that reflects to them the ways that we have colonized our communities. We should create opportunities to confront land grants and property acquisition, the erasure of Tribal nations, and the elitist elevation of Euro-American research methods and pedagogies. We have seen this effort in the ways that many writing center directors are promoting linguistic justice. Although linguistic justice is usually associated with racial justice, the erasure of Indigenous languages through compulsory English in schools is, as we know, a method of colonization that still affects Native communities. The efforts in writing centers to encourage linguistic autonomy both within our walls and when we work with faculty hold up a mirror to how the academy has weaponized language against historically marginalized populations.

Of course, this is only one example, and I feel limited by my own positionality as a white woman. As I have written and revised this chapter, I have learned more about opportunities to decolonize my writing center than I had originally considered available. In part, I argue, this is because the academy often silos us into units, disrupting the ease of building communities, engaging in collaboration, and conspiring to dismantle oppression. We become so mired in our individual departments and work that we cannot meet with others to share and compare what we are seeing and experiencing, gain new insights from others, support colleagues and community members, and so on.

I urge WCAs to collaborate with other decolonial pedagogues on campus to challenge their colleagues to reflect on and end colonial practices. We need to create more possibilities, in other words. I have done this on my campus by working closely with the Center for Teaching Excellence, hosting workshops and the inaugural master class series on pedagogy. I have started my work by focusing on linguistic justice, and I plan to propose workshops that cast increasing attention on neoliberal, capitalist pedagogies and offer ways to resist these structures. I have faced pushback from anonymous evaluations that have criticized my attention on linguistic injustice and racism. For example, critics uncomfortable with my approaches to linguistic justice in academic writing have wondered if students coming from my courses or the Writing Center will be prepared to write in the workplace. This kind of criticism assumes that writing has a single standard that academics alone understand, employ, and teach. But as Jennifer Martin, a writing center tutor at a Tribal college and contributor to *Writing Centers and Racial Justice: A Guidebook for Critical Praxis*, reminds us, white academics do not own good communication, but opposition to linguistic justice creates barriers to reciprocal relationships between communicator and listener and limits the rhetorical approaches to narrative, argument, and epistemology (20–22). Facing criticism from tenured colleagues when I am not on the tenure track terrifies me, but it is listening to colleagues like Martin that reminds me that I have an obligation to continue to push both myself and my campus toward more equitable teaching practices.

Finally, I suggest something that I have not yet done—moving the center outside the academy into the community. This idea, while well-meaning, could have unintended consequences, which is why I have not yet piloted a community communication center. I do not want to increase the circumference of colonization. Instead, I imagine a place where writers and communicators from all backgrounds come together to teach and learn as a community with the goal of increasing justice and agency for the most resilient communities. I find it helpful to look at some of the work Beth Godbee is doing with Heart-Head-Hands, her business in which she brings justice-oriented writing and justice-*doing* education into public spaces (Heart-Head-Hands). Godbee has offered writing courses in public libraries ("Contemplative Writing"), often in collaboration with colleagues such as Eric Darnell Pritchard and the University of Arkansas's Community Literacies Collaboratory ("Community Literacies Collaboratory"). Rather than bringing traditional academic writing to the public, Godbee (with Pritchard's support as the Brown Chair in English Literacy) offers a series of workshops that ask participants to consider the ways that writing can and does have real consequences ("Contemplative Writing"). The goal is not to change writers or their writing (often a goal of writing centers), but to situate writing as a practice and action with real-world stakes, both personal and civic. Through the series, Godbee asks questions of both herself and the participants rather than entering a public space claiming to have answers. The only assumption is that writing is meaningful, one that writers from all backgrounds could share.

I feel comfortably uncomfortable in my position as a white woman to imagine what a decolonial community writing center would or should look like and how it might operate, as I worry about stepping into a situation and further harming the Indigenous people despite my good intentions. When I consider the possibilities, I am aware that I could slide into the white savior trope, which is simply another approach to colonizing communities. But it is worthwhile attempting to understand what a decolonial center that moves out of the academy and into the community might be informed by, specifically the values that undergird pedagogy and relationships. Thomas Deans writes about his experience at the University of Connecticut's Writing Center, where a program that started as outreach transitioned into a network (92). What started as a "binary partnership" in which writing tutors entered one secondary school turned into a cooperative effort to teach and train peer tutors at schools across the region: "We maintained our engagement with secondary schools but shifted focus from delivering tutoring at one school to building regional capacity for middle and high schools to start and sustain their own peer writing centers" (93). These center staffs meet annually at a conference to learn from one another. I imagine a decolonial writing center could look like this: Rather than reach out to a school—thus keeping writing tutoring within a traditional academic space—I would reach out to a local community center to work with, beginning a partnership that would start with tutors working with clients there while also training interested tutors from within the community. Eventually, the community tutors would take over the care and management of the writing center, although the original writing center's WCA and tutors would remain open and available for support.

However, Anis Bawarshi and Stephanie Pelkowski's warning about acculturation must be addressed in the ways that the originating writing center enters the space, tutors clients, and prepares other tutors. Bawarshi and Pelkowski call for tutors to "adopt a critical consciousness" of the "epistemological demands [of] the university" (44). In this imagined writing center, tutors would need to be aware of the ways they may unconsciously colonize a community space through their presence and practice by bringing academia into the community setting and imposing white, hegemonic writing practices on this new site. In training before and during their time in the community space, they should create a center that

> should become a site in which marginalized [writers] can become critically conscious of how and why academic discourses construct various subject positions so that [writers] . . . [may] recognize and contend with the threat to their home subject positions—their racial, class-based, gendered points of view and experiences—resulting from their mastery of academic discourses. (50)

The goal is not to take over voices, change writers, or even change the community; rather, it is to work together to add more skills to a community's metaphorical toolbox as they navigate their various rhetorical situations. In other words, the tutors in the community center would create what Bawarshi and Pelkowski call a "contact zone" where tutors and writers have direct conversations about the way white writing standards affect the writers and where writers maintain agency in a linguistic system that has sought to erase them (52–53).

Empowerment, when used by well-meaning white people, I argue, is closely related to emancipation and, therefore, to Mignolo's critique of liberation as a product of colonial logic (455). The idea here is to recognize the power within people from marginalized backgrounds and to offer a space where locals can work together toward building the community that is their home. *They* create a space that challenges who accesses and uses higher education while also making space for projects that challenge the power structures of our communities. I do not yet know what this looks like in practice, but there are some writing centers, like the one at Michigan State University, that we can look to for guidance. The writing center can offer resources, tutor-teachers, and even space for the public to work and have access to the university. We can at least begin to consider how we are hoarding our skills and knowledge from the people we have historically excluded from the university.

CONCLUSION

I am imperfect as a WCA seeking to decolonize her thinking, her pedagogy, and her writing center. Tutors have rightly called me out when I lapsed into colonial ways of setting up our space or thinking of tutoring. Perhaps that—being comfortable with tutors criticizing a WCA publicly—is the most important strategy I can suggest in my toolbox. I want to say here, at the end, that I am not offering what I do as a definitive answer to decolonizing the writing center. In fact, these are at most first steps, and I am not the only WCA taking them. There are additional models built by Marilee Brooks-Gillies ("Constellations"; *Crafting Place*), Trixie G. Smith, and other WCAs who have worked longer to decolonize their centers and campuses than I have. Given how we must tailor any approach to our own campus, I have offered here some reflections on how this white, cis WCA has begun her own work of decolonization in the writing center space. I intend this chapter to make WCAs and tutors uncomfortable with our practices, pedagogy, spaces, and roles. I want us to question whether we offer safety or just violence in a nicer package. I argue that it is the latter, and that we have an obligation and the privilege because of our liminal space on college campuses to become something better, not by looking inward, not just by inviting in BIPOC tutors and students, but by turning outward and learning from what decolonial practices can teach us. Most important, I argue for radical honesty about what writing centers are teaching when tutors help writers.

NOTE

1. I want to note that I am not here to discuss who is or isn't authentically Indigenous.

WORKS CITED

Bawarshi, Anis, and Stephanie Pelkowski. "Postcolonialism and the Idea of a Writing Center." *The Writing Center Journal,* vol. 19, no. 2, Spring/Summer 1999, pp. 41–58.

Brooks-Gillies, Marilee. "Constellations across Cultural Rhetorics and Writing Centers." *The Peer Review,* vol. 2, no. 1, Spring 2018, http://thepeerreview-iwca.org/issues/relationality-si/constellations-across-cultural-rhetorics-and-writing-centers/.

———. *Crafting Place: Rhetorical Practices of the Everyday.* Michigan State University, 2013, Doctoral dissertation.

"Community Literacies Collaboratory." *University of Arkansas,* Fulbright College of Arts & Sciences, https://english.uark.edu/graduate/brown-chair-in-english-literacy/community_literacies_collaboratory.php. Accessed 21 June 2024.

Deans, Thomas. "A Network Approach to Writing Center Outreach." *Community Literacy Journal,* vol. 15, no. 1, Spring 2021, pp. 92–96.

Faison, Wonderful, and Anna Treviño. "Race, Retention, Language, and Literacy: The Hidden Curriculum of the Writing Center." *The Peer Review,* vol. 1, no. 2, Fall 2017, http://thepeerreview-iwca.org/issues/braver-spaces/race-retention-language-and-literacy-the-hidden-curriculum-of-the-writing-center/.

Godbee, Beth. "Contemplative Writing: Journaling and Other Practices for Reflection, Mindfulness, and Intentionality." *Heart-Head-Hands,* 1 Oct. 2021, https://heart-head-hands.com/contemplative-writing-journaling/.

———. *Heart-Head-Hands: Everyday Living for Justice.* 2024, https://heart-head-hands.com/.

Martin, Jennifer. "Tutoring and Practice at a Tribal College." *Writing Centers and Racial Justice: A Guidebook for Critical Praxis,* edited by Talisha Haltiwanger Morrison and Deidre Anne Evans Garriott, Utah State UP, 2023, pp. 15–30.

Mbembe, Achille Joseph. "Decolonizing the University: New Directions." *Arts and Humanities in Higher Education,* vol. 15, no. 1, 2016, pp. 29–45.

McKinney, Jackie Grutsch. *Peripheral Visions for Writing Centers.* Utah State UP, 2013.

Mignolo, Walter D. "Delinking: The Rhetoric of Modernity, the Logic of Coloniality and the Grammar of De-coloniality." *Globalization and the De-Colonial Option*, special issue of *Cultural Studies*, vol. 21, no. 2–3, 2007, pp. 449–514.

Powell, Malea. "2012 CCCC Chair's Address: Stories Take Place—A Performance in One Act." *College Composition and Communication,* vol. 64, no. 2, 2012, pp. 383–406.

Powell, Malea, et al. "Our Story Begins Here: Constellating Cultural Rhetorics." *Enculturation* 25 Oct. 2014, https://enculturation.net/our-story-begins-here.

Smith, Trixie G. "'Oh, I Get By with a Little Help from My Friends': Short-Term Writing Center/Community Collaborations." *WAC Partnerships between Secondary and Postsecondary Institutions,* edited by Jacob S. Blumner and Pamela B. Childers, WAC Clearinghouse and Parlor Press, 2016. pp. 155–66.

University of South Carolina. "Enrollment Overview Dashboard." Office of Institutional Research, Assessment, and Analytics, https://sc.edu/about/offices_and_divisions/institutional_research_assessment_and_analytics/uofsc_data_dashboards/enrollment/overview.php. Accessed 13 Jan. 2025.

Young, Vershawn Ashanti. "'Nah, We Straight': An Argument against Code Switching." *JAC,* vol. 29, no. 1/2, 2009, pp. 49–76.

Chapter 7

Invisibility and Colonial Logics: Narrative Reframing of Indigenous Presence on Campus

Lisa King
University of Tennessee, Knoxville

I'VE STOPPED COUNTING HOW MANY times I hear these stories from the Indigenous students on our campus: an Indigenous student overhears a conversation making fun of Indigenous peoples, particularly local Tribes; a professor fails to acknowledge, even in the most obvious of circumstances, that Indigenous peoples are still here, with an Indigenous student sitting right in front of them; feeling unseen and unmoored, Indigenous students feel more homesick than ever, and they want to go home. The cumulative weight of these moments only grows, but we know that universities were never made for Indigenous peoples. The traumatic legacy of residential schools is ever present—recall that starting with the Indian Civilization Act of 1819, boarding schools were weaponized to assimilate Indigenous children and erase Indigenous languages and cultures (Child; "Secretary Haaland"). The United States is only barely beginning to grapple with this history in a visible way with the publication of the first report on Indigenous boarding schools in the US (Newland). While education can mean opportunity, given the historical trauma that Indigenous communities still feel today, it can just as easily signify continued loss.

Too often the goal of educating Indigenous peoples, characterized by Richard Pratt's oft-paraphrased notion of "killing the Indian to save the man," has arguably changed shape toward something closer to "ignore the Indian or provide token recognition while maintaining Euro-American education's narrow purviews." The double resonance of opportunity and loss is still present when contemporary Indigenous students and faculty find their work, their ways of knowing, and their very presence erased on the campuses that promise education and the opportunity to share what they know; university systems were originally designed with white, cishet men in mind, and those structural assumptions linger. Rhetoric and writing classes are one of the spaces in which those assumptions and colonial logics are still frequently rooted. When Joyce Rain Anderson, Rose Gubele, and I set out to bring together the work of Conference on College Composition and Communication (CCCC) American Indian Caucus members, we hoped that *Survivance, Sovereignty, and Story: Teaching American Indian Rhetorics* would begin conversations about interventions in these logics. In many ways, I find myself continuing that conversation by taking up the same questions again nearly a decade later about how we can identify the larger patterns of colonial logics at work on our campuses. How can we draw student, instructor, and administrator attention to what they do not know or recognize about Native peoples? What assumptions or narratives are at work that prevent that recognition? And how can we reveal how those assumptions and their connected structures operate in our own institutions, and with what new narrative can we challenge them?

In this essay, I use these questions to help me tell stories about attempting to make and hold Indigenous space at the institution where I work. Invisibility and discrimination are grounded in the very stories we tell about Indigenous peoples at our institutions, starting with "there are no Indians here." While my experiences aren't exhaustive, I hope they can suggest strategies to identify moments when accomplices can intervene and hold space, particularly for Indigenous students, by consciously rhetorically reframing colonial stories and modeling what delinking from those colonial logics might look like. This should in turn lead to active efforts to make material changes based on the new narratives.

WHAT DOES IT MEAN TO DECOLONIZE? THE NUTSHELL

Before I go further, I want to address what I mean by decolonial work: if we think about it as delinking, opening up new options that do not depend on colonizing ways of thinking and that enact a plurality of knowledges and options, then new possibilities emerge rather than dependence on the same colonizing systems (Mignolo and Walsh). As I proceed, then, I take seriously Eve Tuck and K. Wayne Yang's assertion that *decolonization* is not a buzzword or trend for education and should have tangible consequences; I remember Linda Tuhiwai Smith's call for research models with and by Indigenous peoples to reflect Indigenous communities' movement toward self-determination; I think of Shawn Wilson's reflections on what an Indigenous research paradigm can and should be, recognizing ontologies, epistemologies, methodologies, and axiologies as a circular process that keeps "respect, reciprocity, and responsibility" at its core (77). And in the context of this discussion, Walter Mignolo is useful again as he defines decoloniality as "ending the pretense of Westernizing the world" and its accompanying narratives that center Europe (Mignolo; Mignolo and Walsh). "Healing the colonial wound" daily inflicted by these narratives and

> escaping from mental slavery (delinking) is the way to escape coloniality. However, escaping coloniality doesn't mean that from one week to the next you would be totally free from coloniality. No, it is a long process and for that border thinking, doing and leaving is of the essence. So escaping means that you began to embody what modernity taught you to despise. And what you embodied that was despised depends on where you are living the experience of coloniality. (Mignolo and Walsh)

This returns us to the popular narratives that continue to paint Indigenous peoples as invisible or living stereotypes, based on the Eurocentric narratives of modernity. These are the narratives that live on our campuses and that the Reclaiming Native Truth

(RNT) project seeks to change. In the following, I outline how this narrative of invisibility currently functions on my campus and make suggestions based on RNT's "Changing the Narrative" guide. Perhaps in this way, we can begin to see a plurality of knowledges and ways of being as a new home to make on "campus" lands.

THE IMPORTANCE OF PLACE AND PEOPLES

The university I work at is situated on land to which eleven federally recognized Tribes have connection: Absentee Shawnee Tribe of Oklahoma, the Alabama-Coushatta Tribe of Texas, the Cherokee Nation of Oklahoma, the Coushatta Tribe of Louisiana, the Eastern Band of Cherokee Indians, the Eastern Shawnee Tribe of Oklahoma, the Kialegee Tribal Town, the Muscogee (Creek) Nation of Oklahoma, the Shawnee Tribe, the Thlopthlocco Tribal Town, and the United Keetoowah Band of Cherokee Indians of Oklahoma. The nearest of these is the Eastern Band of Cherokee Indians (EBCI), just across the Tennessee–North Carolina border. Many of the Indigenous students at my institution are EBCI, but we have welcomed Indigenous students from around the United States and Mexico as well. It should also be noted that the University of Tennessee, Knoxville (UTK) is a land-grant institution that was kept alive by the Morrill Act, and as such, received monies in 1869 from the sale of Indigenous lands west of the Mississippi that has had a 39:1 return over the years (Lee et al.). By the university's own accounting, it very well could have collapsed without this aid. In short, this institution is built on and with Indigenous lands.

But of the nearly 30,000 students on campus, in 2018 only 63[1] were listed as Indigenous (Lee et al.), Tennessee recognizes no federally recognized Tribes, and the university itself has off and on maintained a single memorandum of understanding with one Tribal Nation, the EBCI, that isn't particularly well known or publicized. It is a predominantly white campus in the South, and while it struggles publicly to reckon with Black histories of this place, it does very little to consistently and publicly acknowledge Indigenous peoples.

Some individual courses and faculty do some work on and with Indigenous peoples and histories, but there is nothing to unify them across campus. Over the past decade I've been here, the small size of the organization and institutional barriers and changes have made it difficult for the Native American Student Association (NASA) to keep itself alive and make itself visible and accessible on campus (see Andrea and Belinda's discussion in Chapter 10 for further insight into how this can work). Over the years, NASA has organized itself with some success, but the work also frequently drains the small group of students and faculty advisors supporting these efforts. NASA successfully advocated for a room of its own so that it had more than a mailbox as a contact point, but getting dedicated space on campus would not have happened if Joy Harjo, who was on faculty at UTK at the time, had not leveraged her influence and negotiated for us. It literally took an Indigenous celebrity and future poet laureate of the United States to move people to action. Since then we've had limited access to the room because of door-key policies in the building the room is located in. (It should be noted that at the time of final revisions to this chapter in 2024, the university has taken the room from NASA with no plans to replace it.) NASA has organized a football half-time show with the university marching band to showcase regional dancers and Indigenous pride, but this was an event that took an enormous amount of planning on behalf of the NASA students, and because of the personal and monetary cost and the fact that all involved university parties leaned too hard on the handful of Native students to pull the project forward, we have not been able to replicate the event. Recently, NASA has been cultivating two beds at the University Grow Lab with native plants and Indigenous agricultural knowledges; partly as a result of COVID-19 and partly because of the door-key policies on the NASA room, we found meeting and growing things together outside to be far easier as a way to get together, though our ability to meet is always dependent on the weather, and the Grow Lab is on the far edge of campus for most students.

Figure 7.1. The Three Sisters bed at the UTK Grow Lab, June 2022. Photo courtesy of the author.

Finally, NASA continues to organize regular annual Native American Heritage Month events, though once again this takes resources and planning power. Because the rules for what constitutes an official student organization have changed repeatedly with little notice, the Native American Student Association has been wiped from the university website in the last several years without alerting NASA leadership at the time, thus making it even harder for other students to find us and depriving NASA of the power to apply for many event funds. While the Office of Multicultural Student Life has offered essential support for event planning in the past few years, for Native American Heritage Month in particular, building a community for Indigenous students remains difficult.

If we want to know how the university imagines "the Indian," a quick search in 2022 on my university's website using terms such as *Native American*, *American Indian*, *Cherokee*, *Creek*, and *Muscogee Creek* brought up only special library collections, museums, and place names, but nothing indicating a current or living relationship with the EBCI or any other Indigenous community. Sometimes past events sponsored by the Native American Student Association came up. Somewhat encouragingly, the work of four faculty members showed up: Joy Harjo, Julie Reed, Brooke Bauer, and myself, though both Joy and Julie have since left UTK. The EBCI has some representation with the "Cherokee" search, and the very first Cherokee language course (being offered now as I write in June 2022) did come up, though generic "Cherokee" place names around Knoxville still took precedence, resulting in a sense of "Cherokee" as an idea being everywhere but Cherokee people being virtually nowhere. Under "Volopedia," a site meant to be a comprehensive database for past and present student life, very little came up for Indigenous peoples, and "Cherokee Tribe" actually is the name of a red-face pep club that existed on campus in the 1920s. The Native mound on UTK's campus barely showed up at all in searches, and when it did in the most recent articles as of June 2022, the discussion was attached to my own work with the university museum to bring attention to the mound through a developing exhibition and a substantial grant (and it's the grant that's the story, not the mound). Actually, very little exists in Volopedia at all about the mound or Native students or events, and in some ways that's more telling in terms of UTK's narrative about its own traditions.

The message all members of the university community implicitly receive is that Native American and Indigenous peoples are a footnote, negligible, good for publicity, but never a priority. This story has to change.

DOING THE DECOLONIAL WORK AND CHANGING THE NARRATIVE

Reclaiming Native Truth is an Indigenously led initiative begun in 2016 to "foster cultural, social, and policy change by empowering Native Americans to counter discrimination, invisibility, and the dominant narratives that limit Native opportunity, access to justice, health, and self-determination . . . [and] to move hearts and minds toward greater respect, inclusion, and social justice for Native Americans" (*Reclaiming*). It is the largest research initiative to date that has explored public perception of Indigenous peoples in the United States ("Changing" 4), and the data it has yielded indicate a "toxic combination of the invisibility of Native Americans in contemporary society and . . . pervasive negative stereotypes" as the most significant force and the major key to change. When, however, the dominant narrative of "Indians are no longer here, and if they are, they are [noble savages, degenerate alcoholics, recipients of unfair benefits, etc.]" can be changed, the Reclaiming Native Truth project has demonstrated that public perception and therefore policy can be changed. It's become an incredibly useful site for me because (1) it's Indigenously led research and I want to prioritize that as a model, and (2) it confirms all the things that Indigenous and allied faculty and students already know but needed numbers to "prove" when taking on administrative hurdles. In Rhetoric and Composition, we've been talking about this as a disciplinary and institutional issue for years (Powell; Haas; Riley Mukavetz; Anderson; King et al.), and so it's vindicating that research like this bears out what so many of us already know.

The RNT project is also valuable in how it endeavors to provide actionable takeaways, and the rest of this essay thinks through what's happening at my institution as a way to demonstrate a path forward. The "Changing the Narrative about Native Americans: A Guide for Allies" document, available for free at the Reclaiming Native Truth website, provides a series of strategies for how positive narrative change (and therefore policy change) can be accomplished. Based on the data gathered from the report, any change-oriented narrative constructed in support of Indigenous peoples needs the following components:

- Values: Native values of family, connection to land, and respect for culture and tradition are understood and highly respected by non-Native Americans. (12)

Rhetorically speaking, it is a potential common ground and shared understanding that can function as a productive starting or reinforcement point as long as those values do not inadvertently tap into romanticized notions of Indigenous peoples.

- History: Research shows that most non-Native people do not fully understand the true histories of Native Americans and nations, are open to learning, and feel frustrated when they realize that what they were taught in school was false or incomplete. (12)

Strategic use of new information to fill in these gaps can help create a willingness to listen and/or act.

- Visibility: History must be directly linked to contemporary life. This shows two things: 1) that Native Americans' cultures and contributions are vital parts of *modern* life [emphasis mine], and 2) that injustices continue today. (12)

Without understanding Indigenous peoples' contributions and fights against injustice, it is all too easy to fall back on stereotypes. Understanding the impact of Indigenous presence today builds both the exigency and the need to speak now.

- Call to Action: The other essential piece of the narrative is a strong call to action or request for people to do something. It will vary depending on the audience and the issue, but it should be clear, specific, and inviting. (12)

Without a clear path to action, it is far too easy for a sympathetic audience to nod along, feel bad or guilty, but not feel capable of creating change. Actionable items and clear requests and tasks are therefore key.

To put these elements into practice, the guide suggests, means identifying a problem or opportunity, making use of all four elements in a way that addresses the needs of the audience by moving them to listen and then moving them to action, and having an action or goal to accomplish.

This is a decolonial strategy: it centers the needs of Indigenous peoples, it insists on the existence of many stories and histories, and it draws direct attention to the power relationships that create conflict and injustice. Its emphasis on action—and if we apply it in Mignolo's sense, it would be recursive action—means its new narratives resist simple implementation and should result in challenging the colonial system, either incrementally or all at once, as the moment demands. And it is always grounded in place and people.

CHANGING THE NARRATIVE AT THE UNIVERSITY OF TENNESSEE, KNOXVILLE

To be truthful, this process is messy and takes time. Here I want to demonstrate my own process and the ways I'm trying to enact this kind of narrative building and change at my home institution. What I've outlined about my institution above is deeply frustrating. But what I can also see is a thread of presence, persistent presence, and an opening for new narratives. As I think about my institution long term and how I can help disrupt this colonial silence, it's clear that invisibility is the starkest problem. If I'm applying the guide's suggestions, then the following pattern emerges:

- Values: How can I make Indigenous connections to land, to community, to tradition visible on our campus?
- History: How can I draw attention to Indigenous histories and presence in this place and challenge settler narratives of primacy?
- Visibility: How can I make clear that Indigenous peoples are very much still present and contributing to Tennessee's and UTK's present and future?
- Call to Action: What step-by-step plans can be developed *and* implemented?

These elements and questions are interconnected, of course, and my first steps have been to ask myself:

- What power, access, and expertise can I bring to the table to help enact change? Where can I intervene?
- And who are my potential accomplices/allies on campus? Who is also interested in doing the work, and how can I build relationships with them?

I want to note here that those who want to work with Indigenous peoples and students in particular have to be careful to think through and acknowledge what their relationships to land, place, and people are; not everyone can do the same kind of work, and particularly those in privilege and power can't pretend that their positionality means nothing when they are, in fact, part of the traditionally colonizing university apparatus. Rather than trying to take the reins and tell Indigenous students and faculty what they need, such power players need to be thinking in terms of settler harm reduction, or developing a critical consciousness that does not count its self-awareness as the victory but rather seeks to "reduce the harm or risk of specific practices" (Tuck and Yang 21). To me, this means figuring out how to hold space for Indigenous folks to determine for themselves what programming, funding, and action would be of most benefit—and then support it, not table it, ignore it, or perform empty allyship for the glory. I'm deliberately using the language of *accomplice* because it connotes a relationship of support, of risk-taking, and of getting one's proverbial hands dirty, rather than the connotation of *ally*, which unfortunately has come to signify more superficial relationships with less substance.[2]

Coalition building across historically oppressed groups is also important. It needs to be understood that decolonial work cannot be simply folded into the larger concept of "social justice" (see Tuck and Yang) without committing further erasure of Indigenous peoples. At the same time, we also know that other communities have been hurt in different and also devastating ways—I'm thinking specifically but not only of the relationship between stolen Indigenous Native American land and stolen Indigenous African bodies and their overlaps in this country—and there is a deep need to recognize the ways in which each community suffers and what needs to be done to heal it (T. King). Mutual recognition and coalition work is possible and necessary, but it must be done in a way that doesn't silence the needs of one group for the ease of others.

In my particular case, working at a predominantly white institution (PWI) with virtually no tangible recognition of Indigenous peoples has been hard, but not impossible. Through the Native American Student Association I found other faculty and graduate students who were interested in doing the work and had connections to other interested people and to Tribal communities, the EBCI in particular. While they were at UTK, Julie Reed and Joy Harjo were instrumental in sharing the work of supporting NASA, working their connections on campus and holding administrators accountable to their promises. Carrie Sheffield, a colleague in my department, always made sure to devote a significant portion of her courses to Indigenous literatures and makes sure to send her students to NASA events. Since part of my work overlaps with museum studies and visual rhetorics, I've reached out to our campus museum, McClung Museum, and found like-minded folks who have encouraged and helped me to think through ideas (many, many thanks to Cat Shteynberg and Sadie Counts in particular). When UTK finally created a Native American Graves Protection and Repatriation Act (NAGPRA) director position on campus, I was glad to find a friend and colleague in Ellen Lofaro. Brooke Bauer is now a colleague and friend, and together we do what we can to support NASA and NAGPRA efforts on campus. Amy Elias and the Denbo Center for the Humanities and the Arts have recently provided critical support, particularly for the creation of the Native American and Indigenous Studies seminar group (run by Brooke Bauer, Sara Ritchey, and myself). NASA alumni are also crucial to this effort, and Kim Smith and Nat Welch continue to do invaluable work for the sake of generations of students who have yet to arrive at UTK. Together, we've been able to begin or assist in several projects on campus that I hope will change values, perceptions of history, and visibility in a way that will lead to action.

First, the land itself seems to be the place to start. For UTK this means actually reckoning with the history of the land, starting with the mound on our campus, the muddy process of settlement and treaties in Knox County, the sale of western Indigenous lands to generate the monies received from the Morrill Act, and the very limited relationships with Indigenous communities and nations with ties to this land. Creating a land acknowledgment seems like a good start (though it is absolutely not the end), and based on the work done at peer institutions, I know that a land acknowledgment needs resources and actionable opportunities to go with it. Right now Ellen Lofaro and I have a short and a long form of the land acknowledgment drafted. Together we've generated enough interest among the administration in our college to at least create a Land Acknowledgment Committee to consider this work, and our goal is to build relationships with Tribal stakeholders in such a way that eventually we have not just a land acknowledgment on the UTK website but also an entire series of pages on Indigenous histories and contemporary lives, along with opportunities to contribute to Tribal Nations projects in meaningful ways. This is a much more involved project than simply writing a short paragraph that serves as an email signature, and the going is slow, but we hope this will be an opportunity to shift values, call the university's many constituents in to align their work better with Indigenous peoples and histories, and refuse the erasure that currently exists in all the other university's public histories of itself.

The mound too is deserving of better recognition and is a key focal point. It is the oldest human-made structure on campus (not Ayres Hall at the top of the hill) and to my mind a key to challenging settler stories of "taming the land" or "civilization." While the mound has been protected in various ways by faculty on the Agriculture Campus and in the Department of Anthropology, the "use" value of it and the native plants garden around it have generally been oriented toward their academic desires. Kim Smith's work as the undergraduate president of NASA in 2008 and 2009 helped bring the EBCI's presence into the conversation in more tangible ways, from better signage explaining the significance of the site, the installation of a council ring in the garden (with the EBCI seal inlaid into the stone where the firepit would be), and plant labels that visually prioritize Cherokee language over English and Latin names. At the same time, there's so much more to be done to raise the mound's visibility and interpret its history from Indigenous points of view, especially since mound building isn't exclusively significant to the EBCI, the Cherokee Nation, or the United Keetoowah Band of Cherokee Indians. With Cat Shteynberg, Sadie Counts, and Ellen Lofaro's support (plus that of the new museum director, Claudio Gómez, and several faculty), I've been able to propose a new exhibition, titled "Homelands," for McClung Museum about the mound and mound building that prioritizes Indigenous collaboration, art, and stories. So far we have the partnerships of the EBCI, Cherokee Nation, Muscogee (Creek) Nation, and Coushatta Nation of Louisiana and the backing of our first official grant monies; by developing this exhibition together, we will help establish a new historical narrative on campus and completely shift the previous extraction models of consultation the museum has engaged in. Our hope is that the current Tennessee Indigenous peoples exhibition space can be overhauled on a new, community-based model of collaboration.

But what about other facets of campus life and study? The EBCI's presence matters a great deal here because in spite of the history of removal, there are still Indigenous peoples here and contributing to Tennessee's and UTK's present and future. Can we bring Cherokee language to campus in a consistent way to disrupt the notion of "modern and foreign languages" or "linguistics" as an everywhere-except-here project? Can we link current curricular offerings to make the impact of Indigenous peoples and their contributions more visible to our students? Right now I function as the point person between several EBCI representatives and faculty interested in bringing Cherokee language and culture to campus in a meaningful way; this has been a challenging process because the Modern Foreign Languages and Literatures[3] department has not wanted to house Cherokee language, the linguistics program is an interdisciplinary program and not a department in its own right, and we have no Indigenous studies program. However, willing faculty in anthropology have expressed interest in adapting one of their course offerings to create a space for introductory Cherokee language and culture as taught by an EBCI member, Micah Swimmer, and the first Cherokee language and culture class has been offered twice now during the May 2022 and 2023 mini-sessions, with hope for more sessions in the future. We still are early in the process, but I am hopeful that these efforts will be the beginning of reimagining Indigenous knowledges and visibility on our campus. And if we can do this with Cherokee language, other regional Indigenous languages could eventually follow.

Finally, and crucially, I'm always looking for ways to build stronger and more consistent support for the Native American Student Association. When I first arrived on campus nearly ten years ago, NASA had a mailbox in the Black Cultural Center and that was it. No room, no space of its own, *no place* on campus. (Though we have to give credit to the Black Cultural Center for supporting us meeting there.) Carrie, Julie, and I did what we could to advocate on campus for better accommodations and recognition for NASA, but it was Joy's arrival on campus that tipped the balance and got us a dedicated room on campus. That's only the beginning, though; NASA is still largely invisible, recruitment is difficult, and in the last two years it's been the renewed support from the Multicultural Student Life program, especially Danny Dominguez's and now Allie Hicks's work to support programing, that's made the difference in keeping the organization alive through the COVID-19 pandemic and keeping NASA students from being utterly overwhelmed. NASA is struggling, especially under the impact of the pandemic, but we are not alone.

In the meantime, I can continue to teach Indigenous rhetorics where I can and bring these four elements into my classes and my program. My cultural rhetorics course is grounded in Indigenous rhetorics, I teach my rhetoric classes with contemporary Indigenous readings and use them to help challenge Euro-American-centric ideas of rhetorical practice, and most recently, I've successfully led the effort to change the structure of the MA and PhD rhetoric and composition exam lists to stop centering the Greco-Roman tradition and instead think in terms of relationship, connections, and responsibility. The mound exhibition at the museum is also moving forward, and even if it costs me promotion because it isn't "traditional" scholarship with a tidy monograph to show for it, this is where I need to put my energy and time because this work is more in line with the needs of the communities I wish to serve.

CONCLUSION

Sometimes it feels overwhelming to consider all the ways in which colonial narratives on our campuses need to be challenged, but we should feel heartened that wherever we are, whatever position we are in, there are ways to make change. From our classrooms, to curriculum, to our majors, to our departments and the larger administration, there are ways to do decolonial work and to provide new options that decenter the European narrative of colonial supremacy in whatever forms it takes. The "Changing the Narrative" guide provides a framework and a way to think through and generate those options; I hope you'll take it up.

NOTES

1. I should note that I do not know how this number was calculated; the university is notoriously closemouthed about it, and at other institutions, if a student—even if enrolled as a Tribal member—notes that they have any other ancestry, they may be slotted into a "mixed" category rather than "Native American." We may very well have more Indigenous students than this, but it's hard to know on such a large campus with opaque counting mechanisms.

2. I do acknowledge that the RNT guide is a "Guide for Allies," and as I read it, I understand the use of *ally* as a rhetorical move that chooses that term over *accomplice* because of the more widespread usage and recognition factor of *ally*. *Accomplice* may carry more negative connotations for those outside of academic and activist discourses that have claimed the term for different uses.

3. Now the World Language and Cultures department—but even so, why would Indigenous languages not count as a "world language"?

WORKS CITED

Anderson, Joyce Rain. "Remapping Colonial Territories: Bringing Local Native Knowledge into the Classroom." *Survivance, Sovereignty, and Story: Teaching American Indian Rhetorics,* edited by Lisa King, Rose Gubele, and Joyce Rain Anderson. Utah State UP, 2015, pp. 160–69.

"Changing the Narrative about Native Americans: A Guide for Allies." *Reclaiming Native Truth*, 2018. Accessed 7 Feb. 2020.

Child, Brenda J. *Boarding School Seasons: American Indian Families, 1900–1940.* U of Nebraska P, 2000.

Haas, Angela M. "Race, Rhetoric, and Technology: A Case Study of Decolonial Technical Communication Theory, Methodology, and

Pedagogy." *Journal of Business and Technical Communication*, vol. 26, no. 3, 2012, pp. 277–310.

Hoffman, Alvina. "Interview—Walter Mignolo/Part 1: Activism and Trajectory." *E-International Relations*, 17 Jan. 2017, https://www.e-ir.info/2017/01/17/interview-walter-mignolopart-1-activism-and-trajectory/. Accessed 11 Feb. 2020.

King, Lisa, Rose Gubele, and Joyce Rain Anderson, editors. *Survivance, Sovereignty, and Story: Teaching American Indian Rhetorics*. Utah State UP, 2015.

King, Tiffany Lethabo. *The Black Shoals: Offshore Formations of Black and Native Studies*. Duke UP, 2019.

Lee, Robert, et al. "University of Tennessee." *Land-Grab Universities, High Country News,* 2020, landgrabu.org/universities/university-of-tennessee.

Mignolo, Walter D. "Delinking: The Rhetoric of Modernity, the Logic of Coloniality and the Grammar of De-coloniality," *Cultural Studies,* vol. 21, no. 2–3, 2007, pp. 449–514.

Mignolo, Walter D., and Catherine E. Walsh. *On Decoloniality: Concepts, Analytics, Praxis*. Duke UP, 2018.

Newland, Bryan. "Federal Indian Boarding School Initiative Investigative Report." United States Department of the Interior, May 2022, https://www.bia.gov/sites/default/files/dup/inline-files/bsi_investigative_report_may_2022_508.pdf. Accessed 1 Sept. 2022.

Powell, Malea D. "Down by the River, or How Susan La Flesche Picotte Can Teach Us about Alliance as a Practice of Survivance." *College English,* vol. 67, no. 1, 2004, pp. 38–60.

Pratt, Richard H. "Kill the Indian, and Save the Man: Capt. Richard H. Pratt on the Education of Native Americans." *History Matters,* http://historymatters.gmu.edu/d/4929/, from *Official Report of the Nineteenth Annual Conference of Charities and Correction,* 1892, pp. 46–59,. Reprinted as "The Advantages of Mingling Indians with Whites," *Americanizing the American Indians: Writings by the "Friends of the Indian" 1880–1900,* edited by F. P. Prucha, Harvard UP, 1973, pp. 260–71. Accessed 11 Feb. 2020.

Reclaiming Native Truth: A Project to Dispel America's Myths and Misconceptions. 2016, https://rnt.firstnations.org. Accessed 7 Feb. 2020.

Riley Mukavetz, Andrea M. "Towards a Cultural Rhetorics Methodology: Making Research Matter with Multi-Generational Women from the Little Traverse Bay Band." *Rhetoric, Professional Communication and Globalization,* vol. 5, no. 1, 2014.

"Secretary Haaland Announces Federal Indian Boarding School Initiative." US Department of the Interior, 22 June 2021, https://www.doi.gov/pressreleases/secretary-haaland-announces-federal-indian-boarding-school-initiative. Accessed 31 Aug. 2022.

Smith, Linda Tuhiwai. *Decolonizing Methodologies: Research and Indigenous Peoples*. 3rd ed., Zed Books, 2021.

Tuck, Eve, and K. Wayne Yang. "Decolonization Is Not a Metaphor." *Decolonization: Indigeneity, Education & Society*, vol. 1, no. 1, 2012, pp. 1–40.

Wilson, Shawn. *Research Is Ceremony: Indigenous Research Methods*. Fernwood Publishing, 2008.

Chapter 8

A Story of Parallel Worlds: Decolonial Possibilities Navigating Institutional Spaces

Luhui Whitebear
Oregon State University

> Genocide: European conquest of the Americas. Colonialism: The historical process of conquest and exploitation. The United States of America: a country created out of genocide and colonialism.
>
> —Haunani Kay Trask, "The Color of Violence"

> Non-Natives live in relation to Native people—whether or not they know this, whether or not they recognize that Indigenous peoples exist—as though Native lands, societies, or cultures were theirs to inherit, control, or enjoy.
>
> —Scott Lauria Morgensen, *Spaces between Us*

AS I THINK OF DECOLONIAL POSSIBILITIES while navigating institutional spaces, I think of the ways in which they are created: who creates them, the parameters around them, and the institutional limitations. However, I also think of the ways in which institutional practices are connected to land—whose land we are on and the larger implications this has in working from a decolonial lens. This essay discusses my experiences navigating a predominantly white institution (PWI) as both an administrator and an Indigenous PhD student.[1] Exerting Indigeneity on a PWI requires an ongoing effort to challenge dominant frameworks and paradigms on campus while settler colonial and decolonial experiences occur at the same time. Natchee Barnd explains that "these different spatialities are rooted in the historic and racialized experiences of peoples who experienced colonialism as either colonized or colonizer" (14). As such, the experiences navigating institutional spaces from a decolonial framework will always operate alongside settler colonialism as long as these lands are occupied.

In the United States, colleges were developed during colonial times. Therefore, colleges are a settler-colonial project and an extension of settler colonialism. This reality does not, however, mean that Indigenous people do not belong in academia. Rather, we have a responsibility to critique and reimagine the ways in which institutions operate through rhetorical sovereignty. Lisa King offers, "[T]o claim rhetorical sovereignty is to claim the right to determine communicative need and to decide as a people how Native nations should be constructed in public discourse. The power of rhetorical sovereignty lies in its ability to challenge the very constructions of 'Indian'" (79). In academia, Indigenous people and our knowledge are still highly dismissed, yet our lived realities are very much impacted by it. Academia shapes the future of education, laws, policies, press, and other modes of how we are represented and portrayed. By claiming rhetorical sovereignty, we are able to reshape how public discourse about Indigenous peoples is constructed.

I offer the following examples based on my own experiences to illustrate what this looks like in practice. As I move through them and the ways in which I ask the institution to reimagine its role in further perpetuating settler colonialism, I ask that readers keep in mind that "[r]hetoric is not simply the words we speak or write or sign, nor is it simply what we look like or sound like. It is who we are, and beyond that, it is *who we are allowed to be*" (Price 27). Rather than allow dominant frameworks to tell us who we are as Indigenous communities on campuses, we must ask ourselves who we want to allow ourselves to be. How do we maintain our various Indigenous identities, experiences, and connections to land on our own terms? Further, how do we allow *ourselves* to assert our knowledge systems as necessary and central components of academia while ensuring oppressive systems are not replicated?

REIMAGINING THE SETTLER-COLONIAL PROJECT OF THE INSTITUTION

As I continue to navigate academia, I remind myself that the stories I carry with me are a continuation of my ancestors. I move through campus aware that it was not built for me, but also knowing that the Indigenous epistemologies I was raised with existed long before this settler-constructed society that lives alongside our Indigenous realities. Gerald Vizenor asserts, "Tribal realities are superseded by simulations of the unreal, and tribal wisdom is weakened by those imitations, however sincere" (8). Rather than be superseded by the dominant constructed realities of being Indigenous in academia, we must continually counter these limitations through the assertion of our own wisdoms. This essay is an extension of part of my story and also of the communities and histories I carry within me.

In fall of 2013, I started a professional position at the Oregon State University (OSU) Native American Longhouse (NAL) Eena Haws. One of the first things I noticed was how Indigeneity was framed through the NAL Eena Haw's mission, which was very much based on the federally defined, political identity categories of American Indian, Alaskan Native, and Native Hawaiian.[2] Institutionally, the message centered the space on these identities and the experiences of those who hold them. Because of the nuances that surround Indigenous identity, the mission statement sent a clear message—this was not a space for Indigenous students, staff, and faculty who did not identify with any of these designations. As a curator of a community space, I challenged the story that was being told about the space and who belonged there. After a series of conversations with the community on campus and listening to student feedback, we wrote a new mission statement for the center as an assertion of our rhetorical sovereignty.

It became quickly apparent that rewriting the NAL Eena Haws mission constituted much more than a set of words to define a community space. As Sundy Watanabe writes, "[R]hetorical sovereignty goes beyond individual acts of survivance to an ambitious communitist endeavor. It means Natives having and exerting more deliberative 'say' over Indigenous representation, doing, and being"

(157). We did not wait for permission to change the wording, nor did we seek approval to post it. As a community, we decided how we wanted to be represented and what type of community the space truly represented. The current NAL Eena Haws mission statement reads:

> The Native American Longhouse (NAL) Eena Haws represents the Indigenous people of the Americas and Pacific Islands. We strive to deconstruct colonial borders' impact on Indigenous identities while also honoring the sovereignty of Tribes. While protecting and preserving the rights of Indigenous people, we provide a sense of home/community for Indigenous students that helps preserve their Indigenous identities while in college. The NAL provides a source of support honoring the cultures of the first people of these lands. We also provide educational opportunities to educate all about the region's Tribes (dce.oregonstate.edu/nal).

This rewording became a way to recognize the shared experiences of Indigenous people with settler colonialism, not as an abstract but rather as a lived reality both in home communities and with the institution. The statement became a way to center the impacts of settler colonialism alongside the necessity of protecting and honoring Tribal sovereignty. The statement includes both explicit language around settler constructs (geopolitical borders) and Tribal nationhood (sovereignty). Both need to coexist. While I do not expect this statement to remain indefinitely since needs of communities change, it has become a way to discuss and critique institutional policies and practices related to Indigenous people. This reframing of Indigeneity is shifting the entire discourse on campus.

THE EMERGENCE OF LAND ACKNOWLEDGMENTS

The use of land acknowledgments has begun to rapidly emerge in academic institutions despite being a common practice for Indigenous people since the beginning of our travels to one another's lands. While they have existed in other places such as Canada and New Zealand, the practice is still fairly new in the United States. This is a good step forward for institutions but cannot be the end of the conversation or they become an aesthetic that contributes to the erasure of the continual presence of Indigenous people. Regarding the erasure of Indigenous people to maintain settler dominance, Malea Powell writes, "In short, 'the Indian' (whatever that may be) must disappear so that 'America' can live" (402). As an extension of the settler-colonial "America," institutions rely on the continual erasure of Indigenous knowledge and connections to land in order to justify the occupation of those lands as well as assert settler-colonial knowledge systems as superior. Land acknowledgments cannot be a box to check at the start of meetings, events, and other spaces people gather as a way to honor *what once was* in ways that feel good to those reading them or they run the risk of perpetuating this erasure. Rather, the responsibilities to the Indigenous people and communities mentioned in the land acknowledgments must be put into action. Otherwise, they become another tool to uphold settler colonialism.

OSU has also begun to practice land acknowledgments. What started as the grassroots effort of a handful of Indigenous faculty and staff quickly became a more formalized institutional practice. The current land acknowledgment[3] in use reads,

> Oregon State University in Corvallis, Oregon, is located within the traditional homelands of the Marys River or Ampinefu, Band of Kalapuya. Following the Willamette Valley Treaty of 1855 [Kalapuya etc. Treaty], Kalapuya people were forcibly removed to reservations in Western Oregon. Today, living descendants of these people are a part of the Confederated Tribes of Grand Ronde Community of Oregon (grandronde.org) and the Confederated Tribes of the Siletz Indians.[4]

The statement can now be seen on many syllabi, email signatures, and institutional webpages. Additionally, the Associated Students of Oregon State University (ASOSU) passed institutional legislation to read the statement at their meetings. However, the question remains: What next? How do we continue to move past this form of rhetorical multiculturalism in ways that truly honor the people on whose land OSU resides?

In 2019, OSU President Ed Ray offered a land acknowledgment for the first time at a commencement ceremony. When first approached about this potential move, my initial thought was, finally! However, I wanted to challenge upper administration to do more than just read a brief statement as a formality. Barnd explains that Native place names in Corvallis are more of "a nod toward inclusion. Rhetorical multiculturalism" (54). The significance of commencement ceremonies offered an opportunity to ask for more than a nod toward inclusion. I suggested making a call to action during the welcoming speech as well as providing information about the local Tribes on the commencement program, both of which happened. To open commencement, President Ray offered these words that I helped develop following the more standardized land acknowledgment above:

> As a land grant institution, Oregon State University recognizes the impact our history had on the local Indigenous communities. It is part of our shared responsibility to understand the lasting impacts this has on the Oregon tribes in current times. Part of the commitment to the people whose ancestral land we now reside [on] is learning more about the tribal communities they are now a part of. This can start by learning more about the Grand Ronde and Siletz Tribes beyond our time here today. I encourage you all to take a look at the back of your commencement program to find resources to learn about your local tribal history. (Ray)

While this is a small step forward, the feedback from those who were present to hear the speech has been positive. As with the ASOSU legislation, the question remains: What next? As an Indigenous professional on campus, I ask that question often. Small steps cannot stop momentum toward larger institutional changes.

During the summer following the 2019 commencement, I was approached by the Office of Institutional Diversity to be on a team with other colleagues to plan an educational session for the Board of Trustees to help them understand the meaning behind the land acknowledgment. The politics behind land and Indigenous identity could not be overlooked in this instance: "Native peoples' connection to land is not just cultural, as it is usually, and often sentimentally, understood; it is also political—about governments, boundaries, authority over people and territory" (Konkle 12). There was a quick consensus by the team that representatives from the local Tribes should be invited to tell their Tribal histories in their own words. It was not only the respectful thing to do but also the right thing to do. The Tribes should be afforded the same rhetorical sovereignty we practice on campus. Otherwise, we would be upholding the same type of settler-colonial dominance over whose knowledge is legitimate. The result was powerful. The Tribal representatives shared their histories, their painful pasts, their continued connections to lands, and their current triumphs in continuing on as Tribal nations. One board member shared that before the educational session, she thought it was easy just to read the statement before meetings, but now she understood the significance of the words themselves. As a way to further Indigenize this learning opportunity for the Board of Trustees, we followed Indigenous protocols related to food, speaking, and gift giving.

INDIGENIZING THE CLASSROOM

The classroom space in academia holds a significant amount of control over whose stories, knowledge systems, and practices are centered. Michel de Certeau explains that "[o]ur society has become a recited society, in three senses: it is defined by *stories* (*rècits*, the fables constituted by our advertising and informational media), by *citations* of stories, and by the interminable *recitation* of stories" (187). In higher education, the recited stories about Indigenous people often reinforce us as something of the past, with field-specific exceptions. Our knowledge is often not cited as "scholarly material." I have lost count of how many students were not able to cite stories in their research papers that they heard from elders, their experiences in communities, and other ways in which they gained knowledge. The story academia tells is that Indigenous knowledge is an accessory, not a central part of scholarship.

In my capacity at the NAL Eena Haws, I am fortunate to be able to enter the classroom space as an instructor. I am able to make decisions not only about whose work and material is centered but also where the class is held. Each time I teach, I hold class in the NAL Eena Haws. This is an intentional choice not out of convenience but to remind students in an embodied way that Indigenous spaces are also legitimate spaces of learning and knowledge production. Materials we bring in center on Indigenous people and experiences, but they are also in conversation with the experiences of other communities and/or laws and policies that shape our realities. Student experiences in this space are intended to challenge their perceptions of what the learning environment is "supposed to be" along with the types of materials that can be considered primary sources. While challenging for some students at first, their overall experience in an Indigenized classroom is one I hope sticks with them.

CONCLUSION

Operating in an Indigenized mode of existence alongside a settler-colonial system that dominates higher education is not easy. It has taken a great deal of community support and Indigenous ceremonial practices to continue to push back on the ways in which academia operates. I also recognize the ways in which tokenization can quickly happen to an Indigenous woman in academia. Of being tokenized as a woman of color, Patti Duncan writes, "I was also hired, it became clear to me early on, not only to teach about race and women-of-color studies and to attract and mentor students of color but to *be* the program's woman of color, effectively embodying their commitment to diversity" (43). As the only professional faculty on campus tasked with working with Indigenous students, I have to consistently ensure that I am not "the Indigenous" person on campus. In practice, this means saying no to being tokenized as well as referring people to other Indigenous folk to reach out to. My Indigenous upbringing has always served as a reminder that we do not make change alone, and for me, my way of honoring this truth is to ensure our space is shared with others as we continue to Indigenize campus. As part of our responsibilities as Indigenous people, we must continue to reclaim our places in what education is and should be and ensure that our knowledge is centered in academia. I was taught that we do this work for our future generations, just as our ancestors did for us.

NOTES

1. I am now an assistant professor at Oregon State University. This essay was written prepandemic and is a snapshot of efforts during that time at OSU. Much has positively changed related to support for Indigenous students, faculty, and staff in part by putting the land acknowledgment into action. The name of the Indigenous center has also changed to kaku-ixt mana ina haws in fall 2021, and its updated statement is https://see.oregonstate.edu/dce/cultural-resource-centers/kaku-ixt-mana-ina-haws.

2. This from an excerpt of the previous mission statement: "The NAL Eena Haws represents the cultures that belong to the first people of this land which includes American Indians, Alaskan Natives, and Hawaiian Natives."

3. The original draft of this statement was revised by the Grand Ronde Cultural Resources Department for historical accuracy.

4. At the time this essay was written, there was no way to cite the current land acknowledgment as it started through grassroots efforts and had not been formally adopted by the university. However, that adoption has finally taken place, and the official version can be found at https://oregonstate.edu/land-acknowledgment.

WORKS CITED

Barnd, Natchee Blu. *Native Space: Geographic Strategies to Unsettle Settler Colonialism.* Oregon State UP, 2017.

de Certeau, Michel. *The Practice of Everyday Life.* U of California P, 2002.

Duncan, Patti. "Hot Commodities, Cheap Labor: Women of Color in the Academy." *Frontiers: A Journal of Women Studies,* vol. 35, no. 3, 2014, pp. 39–63.

King, Lisa. *Legible Sovereignties: Rhetoric, Representations, and Native American Museums.* Oregon State UP, 2017.

Konkle, Maureen. *Writing Indian Nations: Native Intellectuals and the Politics of Historiography, 1827–1863.* U of North Carolina P, 2004.

Morgensen, Scott Lauria. *Spaces between Us: Queer Settler Colonialism and Indigenous Decolonization.* U of Minnesota P, 2011.

Native American Longhouse Eena Haws. Oregon State University, dce.oregonstate.edu/nal. Accessed 8 Dec. 2019.

Powell, Malea. "Rhetorics of Survivance: How American Indians Use Writing." *College Composition and Communication,* vol. 53, no. 3, 2002, pp. 396–434.

Price, Margaret. *Mad at School: Rhetorics of Mental Disability and Academic Life.* U of Michigan P, 2011.

Ray, Edward. Welcoming Address, Commencement, Oregon State University, 15 June 2019, Reser Stadium, Corvallis.

Trask, Haunani Kay. "The Color of Violence." *Social Justice*, vol. 31, no. 4, 2004, pp. 8–16.

Vizenor, Gerald. *Manifest Manners: Postindian Warriors of Survivance.* Wesleyan UP, 1994.

Watanabe, Sundy. "Critical Storying: Power through Survivance and Rhetorical Sovereignty." In: Flores Carmona, Judith and Kristen V. Luschen. Eds. *Crafting Critical Stories: Toward Pedagogies and Methodologies of Collaboration, Inclusion, and Voice,* edited by Judith Flores Carmona and Kristen V. Luschen. Peter Lang, 2014, pp. 153–70.

Chapter 9

On Embodied Rhetorical Choices; or, Cultivating a Decolonial Approach to Publishing

Christina V. Cedillo
University of Houston, Clear Lake

We editors are supposed to gauge submissions based on their originality and engagement with the discipline. However, how we determine those criteria greatly influences the discipline's norms, establishing whose research is privileged and seen as authoritative and whose is relegated to the academy's periphery. Whether we mean to or not, editors are always drawing conclusions about who is writing and why, and unless we deliberately engage in self-reflection regarding our editorial practices, we run the risk of allowing those assumptions to decide the direction of our fields without making room for Othered voices. For this reason, I am motivated by decolonial theories and my own lived experiences of colonization and coloniality to make a critical intervention at the editorial level, where decisions are made constantly about the quality and promise of research. As both an editor and a scholar from multiple minoritized communities, I am obliged to weave together the personal and professional dimensions of my editorial role lest I neglect any part of my experience as a disabled Indigenous person[1] working in the academy or the experiences of other multiply marginalized people.

Beginning with what I deem a "Coatlicue perspective," I argue that the backgrounding of publication work ties directly to the backgrounding of Othered voices and that transformation of our discipline requires that we demystify the publication process, thereby rendering it open to critique and change. Coatlicue is the Earth Mother of the Mexica whose head is composed of two serpents turned inward so that she reconciles multiple perspectives, revealing the fundamental connections between all living things; she is simultaneously nurturing and fierce. Like her daughter Coyolxauhqui, the Moon, Coatlicue teaches us to "suture the wounds inflicted by patriarchy and eurocentrism" (Lara 41), two global forces that lay claim to reality by constructing ontology to sustain the colonial matrix of power.[2] The Coatlicue perspective moves me to balance the practical aspects of publishing with idealistic visions of what could be, to support those I mentor even as I wage war on the academy's different bigotries, and to call in and call out others while remaining mindful that we are all related. While other scholars have already begun to consider the activist potential of publishing (Alemán and Olivo; Blair; Blewett et al.), I believe that we can do more. Together, we must expose and deconstruct direct connections between editorial work and global imperial structures if we are to counter violent epistemologies that continue the colonizing work of conquest.

Below, I discuss my work as cofounder and lead editor of the *Journal of Multimodal Rhetorics* (*JOMR*), an online, open-access space from where I advocate for purposeful change in our discipline's publishing practices. In response to some of the blatant racism and ableism disguised as rigor that I myself have personally experienced, I cofounded the journal with Melissa Elston, intending to publish the work of marginalized scholars who have likewise felt pushed out of the discipline. We wanted to create a safer publishing space for those of us who don't often see ourselves represented except in "special" issues: disabled people, 2SLGBTQ+ people, BIPOC, working-class people. I share here the principles that guide my own editorial role to provide a model for those seeking to create new academic spaces, with the understanding that my approach hinges on my particular positionality and cultural history/ies.[3]

1. ADOPT A COATLICUE PERSPECTIVE.

My editorial practice—and my scholarship and everyday life more broadly—depends on what I term a "Coatlicue perspective."

Coatlicue is the fierce aspect of the Earth Mother, who wears the hands and hearts of men. She is the mother of the Mexica war god, Huitzilopochtli, whom she birthed without a male consort. Atop her neck sit two serpents that mirror one another, turned inward to look at each other and forming a single head. After La Conquista, the Spanish Catholic priests deemed her image demonic, proof of the Tenochca's[4] barbarity. While they did not destroy her effigy as they did many other Native objects, they tried to bury her multiple times, and each time she was eventually exhumed (De León 270). Today she stands in Mexico's National Museum of Anthropology but lives in the embodied philosophies of Chicana feminists such as Gloria Anzaldúa and Alicia Gaspar de Alba who see her—along with her daughter Coyolxauhqui, the Moon—as a figure representing Chicanxs' resistance to Eurocentric culture and colonial patriarchy. While colonizer scholars have often interpreted the figure of Coatlicue "not . . . as an earth-mother-goddess, but only as a 'monster'" (De León 273), Chicana feminists accept that monstrosity is power even as the designation is meant as a form of restraint. Women of color are always already the "monstrous Other in the sanitized world of the White academy" because we do not fit "hegemonic definitions of femininity" (Calafell 112, 114).

The figure of Coatlicue should also remind us that her story, like all stories, is based in actual material and physical geographies. "Stories practice place into space . . . [and] produce habitable spaces," just as they "make place . . . [and] reclaim space" (Powell, "2012 CCCC" 391–96). So we must be careful about appropriating stories while erasing those whose stories they are. Numerous Chicana feminists invite us to uncover the "connections in our everyday lives with [the Mexica] pantheon of female deities," but María Josefina Saldaña-Portillo connects this call to Mexican nationalist campaigns that have mythologized mestizaje (mixed-race status) and deployed indigenismo (claims of Indigenous origins while privileging Eurowestern political ideals) in order to silence Indigenous communities (282). She argues that appeals to this "particular, defunct Mexican Indian culture" (the "Aztecs") by mestizas upholds this silencing (282).

That said, several points must be stressed because colonial erasure is multivalent. The Mexica did not vanish, and many of the descendants of the "Aztecs," specifically the people of Tenochtitlán, are still living. At the same time, genocidal mechanisms have long targeted people's cultural connections so that many are unable to identify their specific communal origins even though they know their origins are Indigenous. Diverse peoples were relocated onto one another's territories to foment conflict. Indigenous languages, foods, and practices were legally banned. As in other parts of the continent, adults and children were forcibly removed to parochial schools to have their cultures trained out of them. The point was to lose the name of our community, not just in terms of peoplehood but memory. Thus, because nationalist campaigns have promoted Mexica stories so heavily for their own ends and they are well-known, many disconnected individuals have subverted their jingoistic deployment by using these stories as an entry point for reflecting on personal relationships to Indigeneity and Indigenous communities who contend with oppression the most. In keeping with the point of this essay, the use of such stories underscores care and accountability: just as we can derive wisdom from stories of Deer Woman or Coyote, we must be mindful to never disregard or erase those who composed these stories. We always exist in relation.

Therefore, here I must stress that I deploy the image of Coatlicue not as a claim to a personally connected mythological past, but as a rhetorical figure that embodies my own liminality, corporeal excess, and rage. After all, my own ancestral roots lie with the peoples and lands of the Guachichil and Purhépecha, people with their own languages and cultures. However, Coatlicue looks (as in "appears" and "watches") familiar to someone born and raised in a city that straddles both sides of the Rio Grande, that one geographical feature that so demarcates the life experiences of most Chicanxs (what we are all designated in the US even if not descended from the Mexica) whether we inhabit the Southwest or not. She is a metonymic signifier for looking in multiple directions at once from a liminal location while still looking inward, rather than maintaining a typically Eurowestern linear gaze. She represents a constant balancing act that colonized peoples must practice in order to survive.

Being someone who is neither fully United-Statesian or Mexican, Indigenous or settler, disadvantaged or privileged—positionality is always contextual—you learn to appreciate things "from both sides," like standing on the banks of that river in one country or another though it is nevertheless the same river. This is what informs my notion of the Coatlicue perspective. Unlike the comparable figure of Janus, who looks outward in two directions, the past and the present, Coatlicue looks inward, representing convergence rather than assimilation of opposites, much as that river that makes us Outsiders to the dominant culture signifies the double consciousness we must engage as people who know that our belonging is always tentative and never complete. She is a reminder that coloniality forces us to traverse fractures, some of which I don't think should ever be fully bridged. Thus, for me a Coatlicue perspective is not just about creating a "bridge between cultures" or worlds (Lara 48–49) but about knowing that we are each a world, that we are whole no matter the dominant culture's ontological diagnoses. At the same time, this lens acknowledges what W. E. B. Du Bois deems a double consciousness that results from "two warring ideals in one dark body" (44).[5] I inhabit different spaces simultaneously and don't quite belong anywhere, but I recognize the power that my anger and being an Outsider allow. I use this perspective to orient my editorial work toward making room where multiply marginalized persons can share their knowledges.

To that end, *JOMR* was founded in the sort of politicization and radical self-education happening in the working class and the Indigenous Latin American political punk scene to which I once belonged. In this scene, people read decolonial critics such as Ramón Grosfoguel and Frantz Fanon alongside EZLN communiqués, testimonios by authors such as Rigoberta Menchú and Native survivors of state violence, and cobbled-together Indigenous histories of our respective settler-state homelands because we never learn them in school. Theory happens all the time, but on one's own terms and those of one's community. Thus, along with other online, open-access spaces such as *constellations: A Cultural Rhetorics Publishing Space* and the *Anti-Ableist Composition* collective, *JOMR*'s purpose is to contest academia's claim to ultimate epistemic authority while understanding that scholarship can offer much needed language for analyzing our shared experiences and living conditions. I work with my friend-relatives across these spaces to exploit the opportunities that academic privilege provides while strategizing how to break down barriers so that members of our extracurricular communities can also be centered in important conversations and have the opportunity to read and respond—especially when the scholarship is about them and their lives.[6]

Over time, *JOMR* has increasingly (and deliberately) centered counternarratives by multiply-marginalized scholars and those who work with people outside of the academy to effect change in education and our communities. As thinkers such as Stefano Harney and Fred Moten, la paperson, Mark Rifkin, and Tiffany Lethabo King suggest, so many of us have been made to exist in liminal spaces and temporalities, so as an editor I aim to maintain *JOMR* as a liminal space—a place of convergence—where we can create the new and different things we want to see. People of marginalized groups are welcome to propose special issues that focus on their needs and concerns, some even becoming members of the journal's advisory and editorial boards. Together, we all work to break down genre distinctions and center theories based in home and community vernaculars.

At the same time, speaking very practically, I want to provide publishing opportunities specifically for multiply marginalized people because, in our line of work, publication equals a paycheck, and people gotta eat. We write out of necessity that is both professional and personal. Job requirements keep us researching, but we write about our experiences and communities to contest the dominant culture's overwriting of our lives through either outsider stories or erasure. Yet I am protective of the privacy of my communities and I know others are too. As the taxonomic branch of colonial whitestream[7] culture, the academy presumes its right to catalog everything about our Othered "ethnic" experiences. Within this space, writers have the right to say only as much as they want to say; they are welcome to state that their writing is only for certain audiences, whether by declaring so directly, as do Waziyatawin and Michael Yellow Bird at the beginning of *For Indigenous Minds Only: A Decolonization Handbook*, or by refusing to clarify certain elements of their respective cultures or to speak in academese.[8] I don't forget or forgive the Eurowestern structures of knowledge-making that have underwritten the five centuries of colonization that have harmed me and mine down to the bone. Through sheer necessity, I've had to compose a special kind of disidentification, a refusal to position myself wholly within or outside of the academy (Muñoz). Instead, like Coatlicue, I turn inward all of the perspectives I've had to develop, balance, and maintain, to reflect unceasingly on how best to use my praxes in service of others. This standpoint, based on a convergence of concerns, informs the other principles explained in the following sections.

2. PREPARE TO EDIT FROM BELOW.

Guided by the love and rage that Coatlicue represents, I have deliberately reenvisioned my role as a journal editor—as a collaborator and conspirator with communities rather than an academic gatekeeper. Because of my intimate familiarity with the social and epistemic taxonomies imposed on me and other people from colonized populations, I want to provide a publishing venue where diverse members of the discipline feel acknowledged in their fully embodied brilliance. At the same time, I am careful to cultivate a space where no one gets to claim an illusory "zero point" perspective by reminding authors that they should always situate themselves in relation to their topic and audience. Borrowing the term from Colombian philosopher Santiago Castro-Gómez, Walter Mignolo discusses "the hubris of the zero point" that the Eurowestern world displays in deeming itself the capital *S* Subject that examines the non-Western little *s* subject (166). The "First World" grants itself epistemic privilege in the establishing of disciplinary research structures, creating "the impression that [its own] knowledge-making has no geo-political location and that its location is in an ethereal place that . . . has been successfully naturalized" (167). From the zero-point position, coloniality distinguishes *humanitas* (those who can cogitate) from *anthropos* (those who simply are) based on a group's acceptance (or not) of Eurowestern frameworks, exhorting those who fall short to strive for full humanity by taking on its schema. The advantages provided by "identitarian and economic hegemonies" invite the Other to turn away from in-group alliances in favor of the "benevolent" order of power (Puar 31–32). In short, this is how the ascendancy of whiteness occurs. Eurocentricity composes structures of knowledge that bolster the impression that its version of reality *is* reality, and we participate in this process when we pretend that our research is objective and neutral rather than socially and culturally locatable. Call me an idealist, but I believe (hope?) that by attuning our publishing practices to the practical realities of marginalized groups, we can re-matter subjectivity as subjective. That requires working to decolonize the harmful epistemologies seeking to constrain us.

When I say I'm striving for a decolonial approach to editorial work, I don't simply mean including the voices of marginalized peoples if and where I can. Definitions matter because colonization is ongoing and real; all universities in the Americas are built on Native lands. Colonial frameworks shape practices and pedagogies, regulating how we (re)produce and consume knowledge. Decolonization and decoloniality mean undoing the violence wreaked on the land, our bodies, and our minds. A historical relationship between writing and colonization contributes directly to the displacement of Indigenous cultures by centering Eurowestern ways of knowing, precluding "a coexistence of languages, literacies, memories, and space with [I] ndigenous knowledges" and marking "what is different [as] wrong or deficient" (Haas, "Toward" 188–89). It is crucial that we work to decolonize our own praxes in concrete ways. I do not believe the academy itself can be decolonized, being the main vehicle through which colonial knowledge and its frameworks have been authorized. My ultimate goal is total decolonization of the land known as Turtle Island and Cemanahuac, using the tools at my disposal to work toward that goal over the course of a lifetime.

Deploying the term *decolonize* without this aim in mind proves more epistemic colonization. As Eve Tuck and K. Wayne Yang remind us, decolonization is not an interchangeable term for social justice work. Decolonization means centering Indigenous sovereignty and the distinctive "[e]pistemological, ontological, and cosmological relationships to land" that colonization has tried to destroy (5); asking ourselves honestly how what we do professionally and personally contributes to repatriation of the land to Native peoples around the world; and holding ourselves accountable to the specific peoples whose lands we are on.

3. SLOW DOWN AND REFLECT TO PRACTICE GOOD RELATIONS.

By now, some readers may find themselves wondering when we get to the actual publishing part, but we must recognize that haste is part of the problem. Decolonial praxes entail contesting the dehumanizing expediency privileged by colonial capitalism. Today's colonial notions of time are based in evangelical stereotypes about Native peoples being idle and therefore sinful (see Smith), and they continue to dictate what counts as appropriate temporalities of learning, researching, and teaching (Shahjahan; Datta; Villanueva). That same colonial notion of time tells us that we should churn out publications constantly even if that means degrading vulnerable writers for "wasting" the editor's or reviewer's valuable time or ignoring our ethical responsibilities to the communities about whom we write. Therefore, a conscientious editor needs to slow down to ensure that they respect writers and the research communities we should be fostering. This slowing down process includes reflecting on the cultural, social, and material networks that we inhabit—the communities disrupted by the presence of our universities and the lands where they stand. Scholars from colonized populations already contend with these concerns before we sit down to work, knowing we have a responsibility to honor our communities and ancestors through our efforts.

Sometimes I wonder what it must be like to skip all this additional labor and jump right into it, into the supposedly "real" research and editing, without having to wade through the political quagmire that disciplines colonized bodies into unfamiliar shapes. Navigating the everyday is laborious when your skin isn't the right color or the language you speak offends people simply because it is spoken. These issues are precisely why I aim to use *JOMR* to make everyday life matter to us as a discipline, even as I seek to underscore the relevance of scholarly activity to everyday life. Even as I know that academia and home communities should remain separate domains if marginalized peoples are to safeguard our cultures. Because my editing requires sitting with people's writing so that, if needed, I can discuss with authors whether they feel comfortable disclosing certain parts of themselves or their backgrounds. Sometimes we feel like we're obligated to give more than we should in order to be seen. Doing this work requires that I delve into an ecology of motives that provides a background for scholarship and publishing, signifies vital issues foregrounded in the lives of people like me, and defends those lives against voyeuristic incursion.

Keep in mind that this ecology of motives is often pushed into the background of our awareness in favor of expedient scholarly production, just as publishing itself is backgrounded too. Publishing can become a functional means to an end, unimportant compared to the knowledge that it produces sometimes at great ethical and emotional cost—an unfortunate real-world example of privileging product over process. Thus, a lot of our general conversations about publishing hinge on whether we've had a very good or bad experience, unless you have the privilege of doing this work—or get stuck doing it. However, we should all be aware of the not insignificant power behind editorial work. As Kelly Blewett and colleagues argue, "[E]ditors must be aware of how power relations operate in a field, be willing to challenge operations that exclude and diminish the experience and knowledge of some while propping up that of others, and be supportive of those who have not traditionally had access to or representation within field conversations" (274–75). Calling for what they term *inclusion activism*, they maintain that editors should use their academic capital to provide different opportunities for participation in our field for diverse scholars at all stages of their careers. When practicing conscious inclusion in publishing, our activism must include work in the academy and the world that strives to ensure that all people are viewed as central subjects, that seeks to undo epistemologies that center the privileged and render others as Others needing to be invited in.

I exhort my fellow editors to analyze the material and bodily conditions that enable and constrain publishing work. Editors (and other members of the field) need to critique the inclusivity of any and every journal. To reiterate, however, social justice-oriented work is the not the same thing as decolonization, which maintains other, more comprehensive goals. Tuck and Yang explain that some social justice approaches may even prove incompatible with decolonization because they erase Native peoples' efforts to retain their land rights, languages, and cultures and champion neoliberal notions of equality instead. That is not to say that measures like inclusion activism aren't worthwhile or honorable, because they are, but to say that we must all evaluate our respective objectives ethically. As Tuck and Yang argue, "[A]ttending to what is . . . incommensurable between decolonizing projects and other social justice projects will help to reduce the frustration of attempts at solidarity; but the attention won't get anyone off the hook from the hard, unsettling work of decolonization" (4). Inclusion activism makes room in academia for marginalized voices that should be heard if we are to provide mentors and models for marginalized people. Decolonization requires working to undo the colonial structures that have been at work on this continent and across the globe for the last 500+ years. Decolonization means grappling with power and privilege derived from those colonial structures at the expense of Indigenous peoples and the Earth, and it demands that all lands be returned to their rightful stewards. For those of us with roots in "previously colonized" lands around the world, decolonization means contending with the structures of power still present after supposed liberation, and struggling to undo hierarchies based in self-hatred, manifested as racism, colorism, sexism, ableism, homophobia, transphobia, and classism directed toward members of our communities and ourselves.

I stress the distinctions between social justice activism and decolonization because I have read research by scholars who use the term *decolonization* to refer to making classrooms more inviting for marginalized communities, to suggest interrogation of the academy's power structures, or to denote attempts to empower students from disenfranchised groups. All of these are crucial actions, but they do not necessarily involve decolonization. I believe that decolonization ultimately derives from Indigenous knowledges and actions, and it includes dismantling the same academic industrial complex that justified the dehumanization of colonized peoples in the first place. This end will take generations to achieve; we may not live to see the damage that the academy has wreaked be undone. Yet we must do the work now for the benefit of those who come after.

4. REFUTE PUBLISHING'S OWN SETTLER MOVES TO INNOCENCE.

In the meantime, the academy remains the agent of colonization's self-authorizing epistemics, so we must contest the dominant narratives that harm us. For me, that means highlighting academia's "settler moves to innocence." These schemes are meant to "relieve the settler of feelings of guilt or responsibility without giving up land or power or privilege, without having to change much at all," perhaps even winning settler awards for their sensitivity and care to diversity issues while nothing actually changes (Tuck and Yang 10). Academia thrives on selling itself as an inclusive space based in meritocracy rather than as a place of active exclusion, forcing marginalized people to weed themselves out when they cannot or will not embody its colonial norms. The notions of originality and novelty celebrated by our top journals are markers of a competitive individualist culture, not cultures oriented toward community, relationality, and tradition. A scholarly ethos often requires using registers deliberately cultivated to exclude public audiences even in research about them. Rigor too often means opening a journal to find an esoteric Eurocentric theory being used to talk about—and talk over—our lives in service to the zero-point perspective. This rhetorical violence translates as issues of anxiety and imposter syndrome, which then translate further into us being at war with our own voices, thinking we have nothing to say when the truth is we're just not being heard. In these ways, journals maintain the conditions that make our disciplines whitestream settler spaces. Editors, authors, and reviewers may not be aware of their complicity in this mechanism of exclusion unless they—we—begin to ask questions like the following, composed to show up those moves to innocence.

Why does this journal or venue do things the way it does? How are its reviewers selected? Who are its editors and editorial board, the real people making the decisions? How do our professional organizations select people to run their flagship journals? Does the journal provide any kind of mentorship or support beyond an editorial decision or reader reports?
The thing is, BIPOC scholars are usually overworked and stretched too thin, mentoring students from our communities and engaging in the diversity and inclusion work universities should be doing, and often we're doing this extra labor for little or no compensation. So this bind may leave us with little time for editorial work, and little volition too, especially if we find ourselves fighting constantly with our fellow reviewers and editors about a venue's valuation of work.

Who do a journal's reviewers ask authors to cite so as not to appear novice scholars? Are these names that are well recognized but only tangential to writers' arguments? Meanwhile, are less well-known scholars ignored even though their work is more germane? Do those names belong to BIPOC, queer people, trans and nonbinary people, disabled people, people inside and outside the academy—or are only white, cis, able-bodied scholars ever suggested? As a reader, does one ever get to read work by BIPOC, trans folks, queer folks, or, indeed, some of those novice scholars who established venues like to shoo away?
We must seriously stop to consider what a journal claims to value, whether "cutting edge" research or socially engaged scholarship. If the former, definitions of "cutting edge" inevitably

> ignore people from marginalized communities who have been advancing certain ideas all along but on their own terms and in their own words; this kind of language easily obscures the appropriation of BIPOC ideas and frameworks. If the latter, we have to question who is writing and why—members of the communities discussed or interlopers who simply enter already established conversations and whitestream over everything. Yes, I'm using *whitestream* as a verb because it is a deliberate action, not a happenstance condition.

As a disabled person of color, I already always have to ask myself these questions as an author before I submit my work anywhere. There are always extra considerations one must entertain as an academic who is a member of one or more marginalized groups. From an editorial stance, these questions invite us to also ponder whether we have the energy and drive to intervene in the goings-on of extant journals or maybe even if we'd like to start a new venue altogether. I know what my choice was, but there is no one right answer because editorial shifts must happen from all sides. In the end, our choices result from simultaneous inhabitance of professional and personal spaces that cannot be left behind so we can concentrate on one or the other. People from marginalized communities usually have to make do, bridging the academic and the everyday and figuring out the terms of this amorphous relationship as they arise in the moment. I believe that these embodied rhetorical choices cannot but directly inform our editorial practices.

People from marginalized communities feel unwelcome in the academy. This discomfort isn't an a priori condition but one created for us rhetorically—verbally, spatially, procedurally. Because of who I am, I have had my familiarity with English questioned by an editor. I used to write in a dense, even convoluted style, probably because I read a lot of theory, and I wondered if white theorists are usually asked if English is their second language. We are told to read Derrida and Foucault, but I suppose we've all decided they get a pass, as does Burke, whose writing isn't even translated from another language. But then, it's not really about speech but about who speaks. As if to drive that point home, that same editor referred to my style's "lexical opacity," because only some people get to use the sanctioned stilted language of the academy even though we are told we must use it in order to belong. That editor refused to send out any article of mine for review, taking the time to write to say that the venue published only trailblazing research and mine was neither rhetoric nor anything new . . . only to publish several years' worth of articles dedicated to the same old logocentric take on rhetoric, specifically political speeches. Running down each issue's table of contents, I often wondered where that novelty was that he was supposedly seeking. This isn't sour grapes but about reminding editors and potential editors that there are real people behind every submission, that we work in a field where we're made to equate publishing with self-worth, and that a term like *cutting-edge* is utterly subjective.

Twenty years ago, Fredric Gale wrote that there are conservative and liberal journal editors, those "who view a journal as a reflection of the community's interests and current conversations" and those "who intervene to lead conversations, determine important areas of study, or 'even' recruit articles that move the field in a new direction," respectively (Blewett et al. 278). I'm not sure these approaches are necessarily divergent. Because in the end, both approaches hinge on who we actively engage in scholarly conversation, how one defines community, and what issues one considers important or marginal. Hence, in trying to make room for O/others, I still weave my professional goals and practices with something of who I am at home and with my love for my cultural, ethnoracial, and linguistic communities, as do a lot of marginalized scholars. I use the memory of my own affective response to said editor's comments as an antimodel. I have to, because I know too well what's at stake—not just an article acceptance or rejection, but the acceptance or rejection of who I am. *Don't we all experience that?* I've been asked, in a manner that resonates too closely with that cliché assertion that we all have intersectional identities. My response is always the same: yes, but we don't all have to bear the same weight of what said intersections (or rejections) mean.

5. GO WITH THE FLOW (NO, REALLY).

There's a reason I began by sharing something of my background on that river; besides establishing presence for me and mine, it proves the material pivot for the fluid thinking, flux, and change that characterize living in a very different stream from the whitestream. The realities of my life do not fit dominant culture models, so my praxes necessarily diverge, but there are meaningful rhetorical, ethical, and political reasons behind any move I make. In "Wandering Rhetoric, Rhetoric Wandering," M. Remi Yergeau asks whose lenses are used to include and exclude ways of knowing that deviate from standard, able-bodied notions of rhetoric. It's a rare and wonderful thing to have scholarship speak directly to your own experiences, wonderful but rare. Yergeau contests the erasure of disability from rhizomatic architectonics that still consign disabled people to linear mis/diagnoses. Wandering is a privilege allowed only to the able-bodied and those who belong, but it is maligned when a person with a disability or an Outsider seeks space in person or on the page.

It's telling whose prose is allowed to meander and whose must remain static in order to belong. In grad school, I asked why certain scholars were permitted to write as they did and the answer was always, "When you're a well-known scholar, you can do as you please." That's not an acceptable answer—though I'm sure we have all heard this same refrain—especially when wandering proves a useful methodology for making knowledge in community. As an editor, I engage potential authors in conversation to know more about their rhetorical approaches, intentions, and praxes. Not every article should be published just because the topic is novel; not every article should be dismissed because the subject matter has been taken up repeatedly. Some essays do more than teach something new—they remind, they reassure, they tell O/others they are recognized in all of their resistant brilliance. When people speak for you or over you, sometimes you just have to talk back. Sometimes you just want to let those who come after know that you acknowledge them. But we can't know these things if we don't talk to each other.

People of my culture will invite you in for coffee, probably feed you, and then, if they don't already know you, get to know you through plática, or dialogue. Pláticas are conversations that meander and have no particular discursive end; rhetorically, however, they allow people to get a sense of one another through a system of cultural signification that reveals much about a person's values and intentions. Repurposed as a tactical tool, "[*p*]*láticas* allow Chicana feminist researchers to draw on shared racialized and gendered identities, communal experiences of disenfranchisement, and existing relationships in order to foster a trusting, reciprocal, and vulnerable knowledge-production and theory-building process that approximates heartfelt conversations between [people]" (Alemán and Olivo 559). Through plática's wandering, potential authors and I compose a relational network of meaning where we can find common ground for our respective goals. As someone well versed in their field, they can best explain why a particular issue matters; I can't presume to be an expert on everything as I make editorial pronouncements. As the editor of *JOMR*, I explain that we aim to be readable and inviting to a wide breadth of readers beyond academia and that the scholarship we publish must situate research culturally—no zero-point arguments. In this manner, we both learn by sharing our stories of how we come to share space. Speaking on the importance of story as an Indigenous and decolonial methodology, Andrea Riley Mukavetz writes, "It is my responsibility to make myself present and transparent and create opportunities for my audience to create and remember stories with and alongside. Additionally, this creates a nonhierarchical and relational shift in how knowledge is created and shared" (6). It is not enough to assert an opinion about someone's work, especially if they're writing about their communities or experiences. As an editor, I want to create a space for sharing that knowledge; beyond that, I want to establish meaningful relationships with other human beings. Pláticas allow me to practice such relationality.

Moreover, these meandering conversations often lead us to places where bodies matter—we do not select directions at random. We go here or there for a reason. Corporeal memory and affect guide us. You'd be surprised and not surprised by how many authors have painful stories to share regarding publishing experiences, especially women, trans, and nonbinary folks from minoritized and working-class backgrounds. Little wonder that we are reluctant to render ourselves vulnerable to editorial critique. Discussing their experiences editing *Composition Studies*, Blewett et al. write:

> The assumption guiding us was that scholarship on race, gender, globalism, sexuality, ethnicity, and ability is vital to the growth and expansion of our field and should be robustly represented in the pages of the journal. But we soon realized that waiting for work to arrive by and about underrepresented faculty and students amounted to magical thinking and that editors and editorial teams can and should be viewed as similar to academic job search committees: both must recruit for diversity. (274)

What this says is there can be no more "business as usual" in our publishing practices. We need to actively dismantle erasing, effacing norms and compose diverse schemes for doing so. I like that word, *scheme*, for its rhetorical and conspiratorial connotations. Colonized Others learn to be protean in our approaches, tactical in our presentation: our bodies and rhetorics deviate from disciplinary circumscriptions. But if we are to conspire to raise one another up and out of the norm's background, we must give publishing's teleology and tactics room to wander too.

6. REPURPOSE THE TECH, RE-MATTER THE PEOPLE.

When I say we colonized Others must be tactical, I refer to all those technologies we've developed to live. Marginalized peoples maintain complex, complicated relationships with capital *T* technology because it is typically "saturated in white male culture—which has real effects related to privilege and oppression" (Haas, "Race" 284). Therefore, we must "challenge the nation to accept responsibility for the exclusions programmed into its technologies" (Banks 39–40). In response to these exclusions, marginalized groups remix, reenvision, and repurpose technologies developed without us in mind in order to contend with and contest those dominant narratives that make us strangers to our own lives. In the process, we refashion our tools. Hence, I am constantly thinking of ways that *JOMR* might contribute to re-mattering those made to feel immaterial.

One crucial technology that helps me do so is the concept of survivance, which scholars such as Malea Powell ("Rhetorics") and Gerald Vizenor explain as tactics by colonized people that allow us to resist and preserve our cultural ways and stories. This technology is far more vital to me than any computer or the Internet. Sometimes scholars forget that "technology" comes from *techne*, meaning "art" or "skill." Survivance is a technology of the body and spirit, felt and enacted and hard to transmute into language. Suffice to say that as a result, I am ever aware that tech is brimming with intent and ideology; technologies circulate, reify, and communicate designers' values. In the resourceful hands of marginalized folks, technologies can also take on tactical value—tactical technologies that bespeak our takes on transformative access, our access to "spaces where technologies are created, designed, planned and where policies and regulations are written" and rewritten (Banks 42). Transformative access lets technologies matter to us but also allows technologies to make us matter. Technology means differently for marginalized people; what counts as technology obtains differently based on how we make ourselves matter as subjects of and objects to the texts and tools we compose.

We have to be cognizant of how technologies big and small de-matter or re-matter people. Crucial literacies still accumulate among "affluent or already advantaged groups" (Vee 207). Our embodied knowledges and experiences must make their way into our tools and affect their distribution; however, they must also be amenable to our uses, our needs. Otherwise, we are erased. The home security system, invented by a Black woman named Marie Van Brittan Brown, is sold using stereotypes that target African Americans. Alan Turing's cryptography helped defeat the Nazis and yet his life was ruined by heteronormativity's eugenicist code. Indeed, minoritized people find themselves in the tech all the time, just uncredited and de-mattered. This isn't to discount the importance of redistribution of resources or educational opportunities. But I think we might shift our perspective a bit.

Knowing that capital *T* technologies come to us already built without us in mind, can we instead celebrate those smaller *t* technologies that allow us to use what we've got? Can we concentrate on finding models of culturally based hacking-invention until we actually see ourselves in the tools? This search already happens in research by scholars from marginalized communities since traditional academic methodologies were not made for us and we compose new ones or bring our cultural ways to bear. Privilege (and its lack) limits assessment of what counts as a scientific apparatus. Yet we develop and deploy praxes designed to re-matter the de-mattered and tenaciously raise ourselves up. For the editor hoping to re-matter certain voices, the "what is" and "what could be" of any tool means everything as you work to compose an issue, a journal, or a field that allows us to matter too. It means (pre)thinking through a tool's capacity to work in service to O/others.

7. GET READY TO WORK.

Despite all these radical goals, you still have to be practical about academic bureaucracy. The job of editor easily translates into another instance when we must explain its importance in yearly reviews or tenure dossiers to administrators who don't (want to) get it. Knowing this possibility exists means "one's motivation must be intrinsically driven toward transformation—a long-term and illusive objective" (Alemán and Olivo 566). But I know that contributors from marginalized communities harbor similar concerns. *JOMR* does not yet have the reputation of a long-standing journal, and it exists without the funding and other resources available through a Research 1 university. Authors may still have to explain to their directors why they chose to publish in a newer online venue. The senior white faculty who typically evaluate junior researchers may be unfamiliar with the concerns of "oppression-based" fields, leading to a devaluation of their/our research (Thompson). I know this well: our work may not be viewed as valid or rigorous if we use culturally specific methods. Too niche, nothing to say to the field at large. It's not objective, though outsiders whose analyses are ostensibly less biased may do it.

Therefore, editorial work means paying attention to people's lives, knowing some of us face harsher constraints due to social, therefore professional, precarity. It means figuring out what kind of assistance authors may need because we aren't all privileged with the same technical and practical training. It means remembering that publishing standards reinforce institutional ones that force us to conform to the norm or GTFO, yet knowing that sometimes deviance is key. It means accounting for the different reasons why people publish, because it's not always about novelty. It means arguing that editors must be willing to work with authors and disputing the idea that gatekeeping equals rigor, sometimes in unreceptive spaces.

Consequently, editorial work is also a lot of free labor dedicated to a field that already demands so much of that already. And yet I feel it needs to be done. Cases like those involving *Third World Quarterly*, wherein colonization was proclaimed a force of good, and *Hypatia*, wherein an author used a transphobic apparatus to justify Dolezalian transracialism, promote rhetorical violence that leads to material and physical violence by erasing real people and inflicting trauma. I suppose I hope to impede such evils with my editorial presence, or at least counter some "expert" editors who don't know why representation matters and therefore cause harm. Which leads to the last and perhaps most crucial principle.

8. KNOW WHAT'S ULTIMATELY AT STAKE.

Editorial labor is intensive and characterized by rhetorical choices that determine if and how research projects develop. These choices affect professional advancement and the direction of a field; they also influence how researchers are perceived within their respective disciplines. A brilliant scholar whose article does not fit a journal's requirements might be dismissed as uninformed about the norms of our discourse community rather than unfamiliar with a specific journal's guidelines. This view leads to rejection of one's writing in the moment, but beyond that, it can ensure that a researcher does not receive the publishing-related mentorship they may need. Such mentorship includes advising people about journals' preferences regarding topics, disciplinary approaches, or genres and having frank conversations about which journals are receptive to culturally centering research and which invite "diversity" if it's presented through whitestream lenses. Sometimes editors fail to remember that a journal's criteria are established by a privileged few over time and that they do not represent or speak for an entire discipline, let alone all of academia. We cannot dismiss this as one person's sheer egocentrism but should recognize this tendency as a benchmark of colonialism since its epistemic branch, the academy, sets the terms of "reality" and sets up scholarship as the domain of a privileged few to safeguard its authority.

As a result, whitestream scholars are allowed to speak in the language of the academy about our lives and communities, our languages, and our praxes, but we cannot do so in turn without taking on the academy's norms. When we take on these standards, we cause harm to ourselves and our communities by incorporating the very frameworks that position us as deficient and in need of saving through colonial edification. Hence, in the barrio we often hear folks say someone is acting or talking white, and in saying this, they recognize both the social mobility and dissociation from community that comes with that performance. But even when we mean *whitestream* as in racially white, whitestream scholars are allowed to speak about us and for us Others, while we must justify ourselves at all times whether we speak about ourselves or not. In "Critiquing the Critical: The Politics of Race and Coloniality in Rhetoric, Composition, and Writing Studies (RCWS) Research Traditions," Iris D. Ruiz provides a survey of research about the active (and actively racist) exclusion that has characterized some of our discipline's "top" journals.[9] Retrospective essays celebrating the groundbreaking scholarship published in these venues list few if any articles by BIPOC, a fact attributable to both the negligence of the authors of these retrospectives and to editorial gatekeeping. For example, Ruiz reminds us that back in 1970, Richard Ohmann, editor of *College English*, rejected work on Chicanx poetry by NCTE/CCCC Latinx Caucus founding member Felipe de Ortego y Gasca (51). Ohmann commented that he would not publish Ortego y Gasca's work because he had already accepted an article on Chicanx literature for publication, written by a white author. In response, Ortego y Gasca wrote "Huevos con Chorizo: A Letter to Richard Ohmann," in which he argued, "Not to publish our expressions or to publish something about us by a non-Chicano is simply to perpetrate the worst features of racism and the colonial mentality that continues to permeate the country" (qtd. in Kirklighter).[10] Apparently, one article on Chicanx rhetorics among many about white topics was sufficient and that the one representative piece was written by an outsider made no difference to the editor.

Today, editors keep repeating these forms of violence. How many of us work with white scholars who write about ethnic rhetorics and are valued as experts for doing so? Meanwhile, Latinx scholars can write only about Latinxs; Black scholars can write only about Black people; Native scholars can write only about Native folks. Otherwise, it's considered odd, not only by the white academy but also by members of our communities who know through experience why we need to protect our cultures from outsiders. That is not to say that only members of a group should ever write about said group. It *is* to say that whiteness grants an impression of objectivity that eclipses the importance of lived experience. Twenty-five years ago, Jacqueline Jones Royster warned us that "interpretations by those outside of the community are not random acts of unkindness" ("When" 31). A supposed omniscient perspective and the right to speak over o/Others are whitestream colonialism's hallmarks. Editors need to be aware of the part we play in advancing these harmful impressions through our choices and practices.

When research by members of marginalized groups is ignored, these writers' scholarly "absence" reinforces habituated impressions of deficit already permeating society. In turn, these impressions complicate the research and writing process for subsequent scholars from marginalized backgrounds and advance biases that resonate far beyond a journal or the classroom. For example, when work by members of marginalized communities is recognized, "the world of letters and the society at large have tended to speak of these moments, quite ironically, as moments of 'rebirth' and 'renaissance'" as though these communities had not been producing art, knowledge, and scholarship for themselves even though the whitestream academy chose to ignore it all (Royster, *Traces* 4). Such talk of revival and resurgence denies the ongoing struggle of marginalized groups by again framing white hegemony as altruistic, willing to lend a hand to these poor unsophisticated Others so that they (we) can finally create something of worth. This talk establishes the preeminence of white Eurowestern culture as (supposedly) intrinsically marked by uninterrupted progress and historical legitimacy, creating the figure of a completely isolated and isolatable "Third World." These fantasies obscure how any "community's material conditions greatly define the range of what this group does with the written word and, to a significant degree, even how they do it," as well as how social forces conspire to draw our attention in particular directions (Royster, *Traces* 5). No researcher is impartial or objective; we all maintain personal connections to our subject matter, which we select for a reason. When we elide such connections, we affirm the reality of those colonial fantasies by erasing the bodies constrained by them.

These conditions affect the praxes of Othered people, and these praxes are not limited to writing but to multiple, ulterior forms of composition: embodiment, presence building, and circulation. These types of composition are all related in their alterity since they're meant to be "behind-the-scenes" labor, backgrounds for the "real" business of academic knowledge production. Yet these issues are fundamentally connected, and they prove highly central concerns for marginalized persons for whom precarity and erasure are everyday threats. Along with the geopolitical focus maintained by majority world scholars, feminist rhetorical criticism reminds us time and again that the "white male body haunts rhetorical practice and criticism," its presence erased when the abstract positionality of objectivity is invoked (Chávez 244). By assuming a central, "invisible" location, the white, cis, straight, and able male body asserts and maintains the authority of knowledge from the zero point. In doing so, it renders all other bodies Othered bodies. Bodies that are all too conspicuous and yet must validate their (our) presence in the academy and, indeed, everywhere. Bodies that must struggle against inexorable constraints to circulate their knowledge even as that conspicuousness works against them. Bodies like mine.

Given all of these pressures and responsibilities, you really have to want to dedicate your little spare time to editorial work. You have to ask whether the professional risks are worth it in your efforts to decenter the discipline's whitestream norms. As a disabled person of color and a member of a colonized community, I know I'm already vulnerable. But my very ontology is wrapped up in five centuries of violent academic discourse, so I will continue to push for change in our discipline even though I consider decolonization of the academy an ultimately unattainable goal—for me, the academy as is can only ever cease to be. But if nothing else, I hope my labor ensures O/others might be spared at least one bad experience based in academia's colonial classism, homophobia, sexism, racism, transphobia, and ableism. That prospect alone encourages me to keep working to transform *JOMR*'s simple website into a space where we can honor life in the margins. And, to hold myself accountable, I maintain that perspective of gazing in all directions and inward, training my gaze-as-action to embody relationship and care.

NOTES

1. In this essay, I use identity-first language rather than person-first language since person-first language can frame disability as separate from, or in addition to, a person's identity. Identity-first language highlights disability as a central aspect of an individual's lived experience.

2. According to Aníbal Quijano, the colonial matrix of power exerts control over reality through systems of administrative order, land and labor, reproduction, and knowledge. For more on how Eurowestern knowledge-making functions as one of coloniality's central supports, see Mignolo and Walsh.

3. As I composed this chapter, I lived in the Clear Lake area of Houston, Texas, built on the historical homelands of the Akokisa and Karankawa. My own ancestral roots lie in Guachichil, Lagunero, and

Purépecha lands, though I was born and raised in Laredo, Texas, settled on an ancient travel stop in Coahuiltecan territory.

4. The people of Tenochtitlán, who called themselves "Mexica" but are usually deemed "Aztecs."

5. Gloria Anzaldúa articulates this double consciousness as *mestiza consciousness*, a term I prefer not to use since the centering of mestizaje privileges a proximity to whiteness, minimizes Chicanxs' responsibility to our Native relatives, overshadows the political perspectives of Native feminists, and completely erases our African ancestry and histories. As María Josefina Saldaña-Portillo suggests, we must be careful not to celebrate a relatively privileged "contemporary mestiza consciousness" constructed through the "exclusion and . . . erasure of contemporary [I]ndigenous subjectivity and practices on both sides of the border" (282). Yet, as someone who, like Anzaldúa, grew up in the actual geographical borderlands, I agree with Anzaldúa that the specific set of perspectives and approaches that I take up are "a consequence of specific experience," that of living on a national(ist) colonial border (Lara 44). Those of us who are Othered must ever be mindful that our stories don't also crowd out those of more marginalized peoples.

6. Beyond *JOMR*, I have worked with Ersula Ore (co-chair of the NCTE/CCCC Black Caucus) and Kimberly Wieser-Weryackwe (co-chair of the NCTE/CCCC American Indian Caucus) as guest editor of two cross-caucus symposia (in *College Composition and Communication* and *Rhetoric Review*) and two special issues (in *Composition Studies* and *Present Tense*) on racism and/in the discipline. We were convened to do this work by Professor Ore, who noted that there was insufficient research about racism in the rhet-comp-comm discipline that our fellow BIPOC could turn to when seeking models of survivance or to know they are not alone, because these are stories that we ourselves could have benefited from as we were entering the discipline. Since then, I have coedited other issues focused on racial and disability justice with other colleagues in the discipline.

7. By "whitestream culture," I mean that pertaining to settlers with bodies that are "profoundly and impossibly unmarked and 'able'" (Dolmage 110) and, typically, cisgender male, white, straight, and affluent. While ethnic, queer, trans, nonbinary, and impoverished persons cannot attain such full whiteness, nevertheless the right combination of identities can grant some measure of whitely privilege if authority is deployed in a sanctioned manner.

8. For example, my coeditors Ore and Wieser-Weryackwe and I specifically asked reviewers for our special issues to consider whether

"confusing" points in an essay might really be where authors from marginalized communities were having in-group conversations "out loud."

9. Ruiz is a former NCTE/CCCC Latinx Caucus chair and the founder of the online, open-access journal *Latinx Writing and Rhetoric Studies*. She has written about her own experiences with racism in publishing.

10. Ortego y Gasca goes on to say in his letter to Ohmann, "But you've done me/us a favor by rejecting my piece. For more than ever now we Chicano teachers of English realize that the only viable outlets for our expressions in this profession are those we make for ourselves . . . precisely because of the kinds of responses Chicano teachers of English have received from NCTE and its Anglo oriented publications" (Ortego y Gasca).

WORKS CITED

Alemán, Sonya M., and Flor de Maria Olivo. "Guerrillera Editorship Enacts the Decolonial Imaginary of Chicana Editors." *Feminist Media Studies*, vol. 19, no. 4, 2019, pp. 556–73.

Anzaldúa, Gloria. *Borderlands/La Frontera: The New Mestiza*. 3rd ed., Aunt Lute, 2007.

Banks, Adam J. *Race, Rhetoric, and Technology: Searching for Higher Ground*. Lawrence Erlbaum / National Council of Teachers of English, 2006.

Blair, Kristine L., et al. "The Electronic Landscape of Journal Editing: *Computers and Composition* as a Scholarly Collective." *Profession*, 2009, pp. 160–67.

Blewett, Kelly, et al. "Editing as Inclusion Activism." *College English*, vol. 81, no. 4, 2019, pp. 273–96.

Calafell, Bernadette Marie. "Monstrous Femininity: Constructions of Women of Color in the Academy." *Journal of Communication Inquiry*, vol. 36, no. 2, 2012, pp. 111–30.

Chávez, Karma R. "The Body: An Abstract and Actual Rhetorical Concept." *Rhetoric Society Quarterly*, vol. 48, no. 3, 2018, pp. 242–50.

Datta, Ranjan. "Decolonizing Both Researcher and Research and Its Effectiveness in Indigenous Research." *Research Ethics*, vol. 14, no. 2, 2018, pp. 1–24.

De León, Ann. "Coatlicue or How to Write the Dismembered Body." *MLN*, vol. 125, no. 2, 2010, pp. 259–86.

Dolmage, Jay. "Writing against Normal: Navigating a Corporeal Turn." *Composing(Media) = Composing(Embodiment)*, edited by Kristin L. Arola and Anne Frances Wysocki, Utah State UP, 2012, pp. 110–26.

Du Bois, W. E. B. *The Souls of Black Folk*. Penguin Books, 1995.

Haas, Angela M. "Race, Rhetoric, and Technology: A Case Study of Decolonial Technical Communication Theory, Methodology, and Pedagogy." *Journal of Business and Technical Communication*, vol. 26, no. 3, 2012, pp. 277–310.

———. "Toward a Decolonial Digital and Visual American Indian Rhetorics Pedagogy." *Survivance, Sovereignty, and Story: Teaching American Indian Rhetorics*, edited by Lisa King et al., Utah State UP, 2015, pp. 188–208.

Harney. Stefano, and Fred Moten. *The Undercommons: Fugitive Planning and Black Study*. Minor Compositions, 2013.

King, Tiffany Lethabo. *The Black Shoals: Offshore Formations of Black and Native Studies*. Duke UP, 2019.

Kirklighter, Cristina. "The Icon and the Image: The Chicano Struggle for Literary Representation." *Pluma Fronteriza*, 6 Feb. 2011, http://plumafronteriza.blogspot.com/2011/02/icon-and-image-chicano-struggle-for.html.

Lara, Irene. "Daughter of Coatlicue: An Interview with Gloria Anzaldúa." *Entre Mundos/Among Worlds: New Perspectives on Gloria E. Anzaldúa*, edited by AnaLouise Keating, Palgrave Macmillan, 2008, pp. 41–55.

Mignolo, Walter. "Epistemic Disobedience, Independent Thought and Decolonial Freedom." *Theory, Culture & Society*, vol. 26, no. 7–8, 2009, pp. 159–81.

Mignolo, Walter D., and Catherine E. Walsh. *On Decoloniality: Concepts, Analytics, Praxis*, Duke UP, 2018.

Muñoz, José Esteban. *Disidentifications: Queers of Color and the Performance of Politics*. U of Minnesota P, 1999.

Ortego y Gasca, Felipe de. "Huevos con Chorizo: A Letter to Richard Ohmann." *Nosotros: Newsletter of the Chicano Caucus of NCTE*, June 1970, bit.ly/2NnKBvE.

paperson, la. *A Third University Is Possible*. U of Minnesota P, 2017.

Powell, Malea. "Rhetorics of Survivance: How American Indians Use Writing." *College Composition and Communication*, vol. 53, no. 3, 2002, pp. 396–434.

———. "2012 CCCC Chair's Address: Stories Take Place—A Performance in One Act." *College Composition and Communication*, vol. 64, no. 2, 2012, pp. 383–406.

Puar, Jasbir K. *Terrorist Assemblages: Homonationalism in Queer Times.* Duke UP, 2007.

Quijano, Aníbal. "Coloniality of Power, Eurocentrism, and Latin America." *Nepantla: Views from South*, vol. 1, no 3, 2000, pp. 533–80.

Rifkin, Mark. *Beyond Settler Time: Temporal Sovereignty and Indigenous Self-Determination*. Duke UP, 2017.

Riley Mukavetz, Andrea. "Females, the Strong Ones: Listening to the Lived Experiences of American Indian Women." *Studies in American Indian Literatures*, vol. 30, no. 1, 2018, pp. 1–23.

Royster, Jacqueline Jones. *Traces of a Stream: Literacy and Social Change among African American Women.* U of Pittsburgh P, 2000.

———. "When the First Voice You Hear Is Not Your Own." *College Composition and Communication*, vol. 47, no. 1, 1996, pp. 29–40.

Ruiz, Iris D. "Critiquing the Critical: The Politics of Race and Coloniality in Rhetoric, Composition, and Writing Studies (RCWS) Research Traditions." *Race, Rhetoric, and Research Methods*, edited by Alexandria Lockett et al., WAC Clearinghouse / UP of Colorado, 2021, pp. 39–89.

Saldaña-Portillo, María Josefina. *The Revolutionary Imagination in the Americas and the Age of Development.* Duke UP, 2003.

Shahjahan, Riyad A. "Being 'Lazy' and Slowing Down: Toward Decolonizing Time, Our Body, and Pedagogy." *Educational Philosophy and Theory*, vol. 47, no. 5, 2015, pp. 488–501.

Smith, Linda Tuhiwai. *Decolonizing Methodologies: Research and Indigenous Peoples.* Zed Books, 2001.

Thompson, Chasity. "Recruitment, Retention, and Mentoring Faculty of Color: The Chronicle Continues." *New Directions for Higher Education*, vol. 143, 2008, pp. 47–54.

Tuck, Eve, and K. Wayne Yang. "Decolonization Is Not a Metaphor." *Decolonization: Indigeneity, Education & Society*, vol. 1, no. 1, 2012, pp. 1–40.

Vee, Annette. *Coding Literacy: How Computer Programming Is Changing Writing.* MIT P, 2017.

Villanueva, Silvia Toscano. "Teaching as a Healing Craft: Decolonizing the Classroom and Creating Spaces of Hopeful Resistance through Chicano–Indigenous Pedagogical Praxis." *Urban Review*, vol. 45, no. 1, 2013, pp. 23–40.

Vizenor, Gerald. "Aesthetics of Survivance: Literary Theory and Practice." *Survivance: Narratives of Native Presence*, edited by Gerald Vizenor, U of Nebraska P, 2008, pp. 1–23.

Waziyatawin, and Michael Yellow Bird. *For Indigenous Minds Only: A Decolonization Handbook.* School for Advanced Research Press, 2012.

Yergeau, [M. Remi]. "Wandering Rhetoric, Rhetoric Wandering." *Making Future Matters*, edited by Rick Wysocki and Mary P. Sheridan, Computers and Composition Digital Press/Utah State UP, 2018, https://ccdigitalpress.org/book/makingfuturematters/.

Chapter 10

Making Indigenous Space through Anishinaabeg Knowledge and Community Relations

Belinda (Lin) Bardwell
Grand Valley State University

Andrea Riley Mukavetz
City of Grand Rapids, MI

THIS CHAPTER IS A RECORDED CONVERSATION between a former faculty member (Andrea) and a staff member who specializes in Native student retention and recruitment (Lin). At the time of the initial conversation, we both worked at Grand Valley State University (GVSU), which was built on the ancestral territory of the Anishinaabeg. This territory was ceded through the Treaty of Washington of 1836 and the Treaty of Chicago of 1821. GVSU is a public teaching-focused institution and a historically white institution. Andrea and Lin met each other when working on the Native American Advisory Council, a university committee under the Division of Inclusion and Equity (I&E) that brings together faculty, staff, and community members to advise I&E on how to support and retain Indigenous students. At that time, Lin was not formally affiliated with the institution and was eventually hired as a Native American student support specialist.

Like any good conversation between two Anishinaabekwe, it ran longer than we expected. In this discussion, we provide the community and institutional context that informs our work. We reflect on our shared work and the impact of that work on the institution. Later in the discussion, we share examples of how we make Indigenous space at our institution. We situate our work in our practice of decoloniality, address the complexity of decolonial work in the institution, and identify our shared goals for the future.

INTRODUCING THE AUNTIES

Lin: Niizhokwe Ndizhnikaaz, Waaganakising Odawa Anishinaabekwe Ndaaw, Nme Ndoodem, Clarksville Ndoonjibaa. My English name is Lin. I am a citizen of Little Traverse Bay Bands of Odawa Indians. I'm the mother of four, and I am employed at Grand Valley State University. [LAUGHTER]

Andrea: Andrea nindizhinikaa, Deshkaan Ziibing Anishinaabekwe nindaaw, Aajiijak, Nindoodem, Waawiyaataanong nindoonjibaa. So, Lin, how do we know each other?

Lin: Well, I heard of you coming to Grand Valley and they're like, "We have an interviewee with a Native woman." I'm like, I don't care who she is. Hire her. [LAUGHTER]

I think I met you right when you started at Grand Valley through the Native American Advisory Council.

Andrea: Before working at GVSU, you began at Grand Rapids Public Schools. Can you talk a bit about that?

Lin: [LAUGHTER] It was quite the introduction into the Native community. I quickly realized that I'm meeting people that are going to be important in my life. When I first started, we had an alternative education program like a high school for our Native students. A respected elder taught there. My own teacher worked for our program. Every Friday was culture day, so we started the day with talking circles. I hated talking circles when I first started because it really puts you on the spot. As an adult sitting with young people, I felt like I had to be an expert. Then you learned your introduction, you learned why you needed to learn your introduction. You know, every day, after going through the talking circle, my teacher would give us maybe forty-five minutes of teachings. And then I realized—how fortunate am I? I get to do this for work. Like, someone's paying me to come here and reconnect with what I had been missing in my life. I continued along that path till I forged my way in at GVSU. [LAUGHTER] Now I get to do the same thing in a different way, for a different institution, for a different age group.

Andrea: What's your formal role at GVSU? Can you talk a bit more about the work you did at GRPS?

Lin: My formal position at Grand Valley is contracted through Inclusion and Equity to increase recruitment and retention for our Native students.

Andrea: I remember the long fight it took the Native American Advisory Council[1] [NAAC] to advocate for your position.[2] One of the worries that I had was that you were going to be contracted to create all these wonderful programs: the orientation, the summer leadership camp, the mentoring program—and then they wouldn't hire you full-time. They'd pass it on to some sort of white settler. I was really scared that what you've created based on your research, your personal experience, your connection to the community, would be stolen or appropriated. That hasn't happened and these programs completely changed our university. Our university is now a model for other institutions. I talk with coworkers and colleagues who are Indigenous scholars across Turtle Island, and they don't have programs like this. They don't have somebody like you. They don't have a Native American Advisory Council. They have a Native student every now and then who is willing to share that they're Native. There's no visibility or representation. If we didn't have you or the Council advocating the way we do, I think our campus would be similar.

Lin: Aw. That means a lot, you know, coming from you, to acknowledge. I think it is the hard work of the Native American Advisory Council.

Coming from a public administration and organizational leadership perspective, GVSU is a great space to become a good home for our Native students. Because of our size, the organization is small enough. At other institutions, the org chart is a hot mess. When I was at GRPS, I used to take students to Michigan State University[3] all the time, because [MSU] reached out and wanted us to come and visit. These students were turned off to the idea of college. If that's their first time ever being on a campus and I show 'em Michigan State University, like, that's trauma-causing.

Andrea: Yeah. I love that you're taking that organizational perspective and making it center, because I think it's allowed us to push through our projects and get leadership on board. I'm thinking about my [work] with the Sustainable Agricultural Project and with the teaching lodge and how there were definitely internal issues. But I was able to get internal funding. The university secured the funding as well when the project was delayed. When I had an issue with another office, I knew exactly who to ask to work on my behalf—like, my dean, the provost's office—and I knew that they moved mountains for me. And I know that at larger institutions, I can't have access to my dean and somebody like the assistant provost.

Or I'm doing the land acknowledgment series, and another person from the provost's office is taking the workshop. She's asking me what I need to meet my goals. I know that she's listening and taking those requests seriously. I hope that folks who are trying to do this work understand that a lot of these projects are institution-specific. It's important to figure out the organizational chart and figure out how to poke at it and find areas of access. When NAAC wasn't in a good place and we were struggling with one of the admin, it was difficult but we still had access to that senior leader.

Lin: Before GVSU, I worked at the Native American Education Program through the Grand Rapids Public Schools; [there,] everyone I worked with was Native. All the students I worked with were Native. I go to Council and I'm in a room with Native people and then when I go to conferences, there's thousands of Native people around me. [Lin is indicating that she told this story to a colleague at GVSU.] And she goes, "Oh, I guess I never looked at it that way," and I'm like, yeah, like six, seven years, I've been insulated from feeling like this, and so when I did go back to students and curriculum [and] would touch on Native topics and such, I had no problem speaking up and defending, arguing, emphasizing all of those things with the professor in the class, but I do see that I wouldn't have been able to do that [as] my twenty-year-old self, growing up in a white community, thinking I was white and feeling like I walked into a room and blended.

Andrea: It is, and we're going off topic, but I think that's okay because I just want to share that I was reading essays from my Anishinaabek Lifeway class and I had them write a statement of relationality and I asked them the question, "How do you make space for Indigenous visibility while being the arms of the institution?" I was reading a student's essay, which basically brought me to tears, and he ends it with something like, "I'm only 20. . . ."

Lin: I was a mess when I was twenty.

Andrea: Same! He literally wrote, "As a Cherokee person on Anishinaabek land, I'm doing this leadership work for these reasons." That was not me at twenty! I was trying to figure out who to hook up with at the bar. [LAUGHTER] We're both trying to make the space for students to be who they are. This is not the first time I've read his work or other Native students' work. . . like over classes, and I can see the change. I can see the growth and I just think that's really amazing that that's happening for them, you know.

Lin: I remember I was doing a presentation for your class, and they were just shocked at the amount of information I could just share without notecards or anything. I said, "It's taken me twenty years to be able to do that. You have been doing it for less than that. If you want to look up to me, you are far more advanced than I was at your age. Like, imagine what you will be able to do at my age!" I appreciate that they look up to me, but the fact is that these students are so much more advanced than I was at that age, and they're going to be powerhouses when they're old like me.

Andrea: I know. I know. That's an Anishinaabek practice though. They're looking up to us as aunties, as models. It's our responsibility to help them see that they have contributions and that we're looking up to them at the same time. We've made these spaces, we invite them to see the challenges of it, and they're responding. When they act, it offers more challenge for us to make it a space that holds up to who they need to be.

Lin: I think it activates them too, to do the work. They've been gifted the skills. It empowers them to want to make change. I remember the first time meeting them. These students then compared to them now . . . I just keep thinking about who they will be in five years and then ten years. It's just awe inspiring. Wherever they land, the work they're going to do will increase our visibility. It's beautiful to witness.

Andrea: I agree. This is why I always end my courses examining how to tend to the next generation. They're the ones who are our leaders, they're our knowledge keepers, and we have to nurture them and care for them in this way now so that way they can do the things that we can't even imagine and hope they're going to do.

Lin: I think that's a huge part of our teaching of humility. Working in academia and finding somebody who's humble is very difficult.

Andrea: Another layer to this is that we are both Anishinaabekwe working on our ancestral territory with mainly Anishinaabe students. There is something special about that relationship. Can you speak a bit to the complexity of that relationship work?

Lin: Since I started working at Grand Rapids Public Schools, I just see such a deep need for people that have reached the level of integral community belonging and institutional knowledge and devotion, that if I were to walk away, it would be hard to find somebody else who would be committed to the work in that specific space. I want to remove as many barriers for my community as I can, and I feel like everything that I've learned along the way is only going to really strengthen the work I'm doing at Grand Valley.

Working in K–12, I really realized how many advantages I've had in life because I had a stable home. [My parents] worked every day. They encouraged me. Like you said before, your parents really didn't know how to help you succeed in school, but they knew it was important. So I think that's that first-gen experience, where my parents were excited to have me go and . . . knew I was going to go, but they just didn't know how to support me once I got there. Also, I watched some of our younger counterparts in community. His approach to advancing the next generation is so much different than mine, but both [are] needed. Both of those perspectives are needed.

Andrea: This was something me and another student were talking about in my office the other day. He said to me, "You know, I came into GVSU thinking that education wasn't important because I grew up around community members who kept telling me it was the wrong way to do things," and then he said, "I took your class, and I'm talking to Lin, and I realize that I need to be here," Then he started talking about [the] Indian Child Welfare Act and how he really wants to be a social worker because of his own experience, and I was encouraging him to follow that. Social workers have done terrible things to Native folks. But we need Native people there to watch out and make interventions, and he's like, "Yeah, I need to go," and he's like, "That's what my intervention's going to be." So we ended that conversation with the same approach.

Lin: I was at a conference once and one of the panelists introduced his colleague, an Indigenous woman who was dressed in her traditional clothes. The facilitator brought up that Native women suffer the highest rates of missing, murdered, and domestic violence. He's like, "She's taking her life in her own hands just by dressing this way every day." I was thinking about that moment because making

Indigenous space on campus is doing the education work so our students can walk around campus in a ribbon skirt and not be looked at twice or feel unsafe while gathering. At GVSU the Native folks talk a lot about the space we have at the Office of Multicultural Affairs, where if you don't appear to present as a person of color, sometimes you're not always felt to be welcome somewhere. There is a current flaw with how our university approaches diversity and inclusion. So it is about creating those spaces simply just for Indigenous folks to be.

The reason I asked you about how last night went is because sometimes I feel pressured to always have a teachable moment in my programming. There are these expectations like we've got to have a protocol. We've got to have learning outcomes. I worry about how my programming is perceived when the implementation of those learning outcomes looks simple, like just sitting around food and talking about whatever it is they want to talk about. I could hear really good conversations going on in different tables and that, that looks like an Indigenous space—them just finding community with each other, problem solving each other, becoming peer-to-peer mentors. So the problem is, where do you find that space? How do you make it Indigenous? How do you get the institution to invest in that space? It takes some of this soft data to answer those questions. In the public schools, we're looking at soft data, and the university wants hard data. This is a part of research methods though, right? How do you get the institution to understand that these very seemingly simple changes can change the trajectory of the success of our students in a quantifiable way that sells them on your work? And that's tough because that qualitative piece is a long game, and a lot of institutions don't want to play the long game.

Indigenous space is having a space where students can hang their posters and . . . have their craft material at an arm's length away and not have to scramble for some random room on campus. Indigenous spaces is feeling safe in a classroom to share what they want about themselves and having faculty understand that not every Native student wants to be singled out or called upon to educate. Like, one of my best students, even when he's in a safe space, he still likes to just observe and maybe not participate. But he has told me that in some of his classes, when they find out he's Native, they want to call on him. So there's the education component of our faculty and staff, to become culturally competent and aware of what they're doing.

One of the things that I learned coming out of my work with Standing Rock and with Shaping Narratives is that when we were occupying Standing Rock, that was the first time I had heard major news stations say the word *treaty*, say the word *sovereignty*, say the words *Tribal governance,* even if it was like a, a four-second sound bite on CNN. And then you fast-forward to last year and we're something else again.

Andrea: Part of this is the ongoing invitation to settlers and non-Indigenous people to talk about themselves as guests or descendants of intruders on Indigenous land and the responsibilities that come with it. I feel like part of Indigenous space too is having settlers see themselves on Indigenous land. This is something I do in my classes through land acknowledgments and understanding the relationship between space/place, culture, and history. I have students writing, "I'm on stolen Indigenous land." That rhetorical move is also making Indigenous space. We're all engaging in the discussion around settler harm reduction. I share this alongside what you said because I feel like in academia there's sometimes this desire to say, well, we can't [make] Indigenous space or [space] for people of color; it's only this one thing, . . . or you're not doing it right. You know, but the reality is . . . that we're all in this world together.

Lin: And that's, that's a tough one to balance. I don't have the answer, but I know that's one of the struggles that I sit with. I want to call everyone in since we're a public institution, but also I need to listen to the community when they say that some spaces are just for us.

Andrea: Yeah. I think you're right. One of the curveballs around the teaching lodge was just that—it was supposed to be a Native space. The non-Native people who wrote that proposal participated knowing that it was not a space they would enter in to. These are nineteen- to twenty-four-year-olds who are like, "I'm doing this labor. I'm using my network to create this space, but I am not a part of it." Again, something that I don't see often in academia. These are the harder conversations to have. Non-Native students tend to get my cues when I encourage them to focus on educating other non-Native people instead of joining in community knowledge. I want students to have a space. And I want our university community to know that we're going to say no and we're going to deny them access to things. But that doesn't mean that our working relationship, our cross-coalitional relationship, has ended or is in tension. It just means this is not the time right now, and I feel like some people get that and some people don't.

Lin: Right. It is definitely a tough balance. I mean, like I said, you got Natives who don't want anyone in. Then you've got white people who want in and to exploit it.

Andrea: I was talking with two hand drummers about our Indigenous People's Day celebration and how it felt really good to have such a strong Native presence. It was one of the first times we've gathered in a long time, and there weren't very many non-Native people there. We got to just be ourselves. My youngest had this huge meltdown because she didn't get a cookie. One of our knowledge keepers, who had never met her, just called her over and calmed her down. And she just went to him. She had no problem going to this Native man who she knew she could trust. And she knew that I was right there. And he gave her his cookie. Like, that couldn't have happened if it was at [a] Grand Rapids inter-Tribal powwow.

Lin: I remember that day too. You know, it was just a great day. I mean, powwows can be overwhelming, especially when they're open to the larger community or when the larger community attends. But that was a really genuine space of learning, commune, visiting, learning, catching up, buying, selling. You know, all the things that we do as a society. But it was all Indigenous for Indigenous.

IDENTIFYING DECOLONIAL PRACTICE

Andrea: So far, we've talked a lot about Indigenizing academia but haven't really addressed decolonization. We've had a lot of different conversations around decolonization. Is there something that you want to share around that topic, or that you want to . . . offer now?

Lin: I discussed this in last night's class because I was asked the question, "What does decolonization look like for you?" This is an ongoing relationship I personally have with that word, in that teaching, and I learn something more and more about it every day. There are moments when decolonization is such a huge idea that it becomes overwhelming. And then there's crystal clear moments when I know how to do it. Your interview on [the podcast] *Pedagogue* ["Episode 93," 2021] where you talked about your syllabus, I was thinking about your assignments and curriculum and having it be consensus based. Like, you can say it all day long, "consensus based, consensus based." But until you have a good, firm relationship with what that terminology means and have solid examples, that's when it starts to crystallize in your mind. And so I find myself always working toward and for consensus without always naming it as such. Again, I don't know if that is because, as a Native person, it's so natural to me. I worry that outsiders perceive this as a weakness or seeking affirmation, because in a colonial framework, that's how it's perceived.

Andrea: Yeah.

Lin: But in our community, what I've learned is that it's not about what I want. It's about how I become the voice of general consensus of the population I am working within.

Andrea: Yeah.

Lin: So it's hard work. It's long work because I probably would have a whole entire plan and implementation if I just did it my way, but then it would fail. So the hard work of decolonizing is finding those moments when it's actually taking place. Because I feel like it's a very abstract idea. But then every time you and I talk about it or I read your work or I hear an interview, I get just a little bit more and more about what that actually means. So when I have non-Indigenous people ask me what decolonization is, I start from where *I* started, which is I had to learn what colonization was. How it was a mind fuck for every Native person, right? Given the fact that colonials made intentional decisions to harm us. It messes with our state of being. All of these things that we were given by Creator, and we've got to fight and struggle to get that back. From the higher education perspective, there are a lot of challenges. One being to get the institution to understand that we as a society, as a community, we just relate different to each other, we relate different to the bigger world, we exist in a different way, we have different thought processes, we have different relationships with seemingly inanimate things that, you know, settlers see. That's the struggle. You know—the hardest thing about decolonizing in higher ed is trying to convey what I know and what's in my heart about the community to an authority invested in checks and balances, budgets and line items, and the silos of an institution. It takes a lot of work to talk to people individually to make sure they understand the cultural logic behind our decisions.

Andrea: I remember how hard it was for some people on our committee to understand our decision to move to a consensus-based governance approach. We had to say to the VP that he can't run the meetings anymore. I know that was hard for him because I think he was taking it personally. But then he realized that we were trying to practice our own governance approaches as Anishinaabeg. To do decolonial work in the academy is to always make decisions that ensure our survival. It's our safety. It's our existence. It's our cultural continuance. It's upholding the sacred.

I feel like academics have messed this up in a lot of ways too. I say this as an academic. We're debating decolonization and decoloniality in scholarly papers and trying to claim certain scholarly paradigms. I'm complicit in this in some ways. I get really angry when I see people engaging in decolonial theory without talking about Indigenous people, without addressing the lived experiences of Tribal nations people. I get really put off when I see people engaging in this work and not being a part of community. Any community. Before coming to GV, I knew these components of decoloniality and decolonial scholarship, but I didn't really practice it until coming into community with you all. That last article I wrote about snakes was my attempt to address this. I could talk about decolonial theory, push out those articles as much as I want, but I need to also work for our community, hold myself accountable, and let others hold me accountable. I remember talking to our university president. I gave her some tobacco. And I was trying to explain to her that you, me, and Simone were not just people who work here, but we are the aunties. Our role is to be held accountable by this community. If we mess up, the president doesn't hear about it. We do. We have to be held accountable. We have to address and be humble in that response. And I feel like that is a part of decolonization. That's a part of the role of doing that work in higher ed, . . . letting the community hold us accountable, and that's what I want to see more of from my discipline and from academics as well.

DREAMING INDIGENOUS FUTURES

Andrea: Okay. So let's talk about our last question. . . . We've accomplished so much since we started working together. What's next on our list?

Lin: Well, my boss once asked me what programs I would develop if money was no object. And, working for eleven years at Grand Rapids Public Schools, money was always an object. [LAUGHTER]

Andrea: I know. I can't even figure out how to answer that question.

Lin: I want to create an Indigenous center. Like, there needs to be a space that is wholly 100 percent owned and operated by Indigenous students, faculty, and staff.

Andrea: All of that: Elder in residence, language keeper, paid tuition, community members can audit classes easier, and a faculty/staff cluster hire. While doing this teaching lodge work, I've been thinking more about land repatriation. Like, what would it look like if GVSU repatriated land to the local Tribes or allowed for hunting and fishing on their lands? What if all orientation packets had a pamphlet titled "Do You Know Whose Land You're On?" And it orients students and employees to Indigenous history through space/place? Or, our academic senate followed through on their commitment to DEI through holding faculty more accountable [for] creating a diverse curriculum that integrates Indigenous ideas. I think we had a big win with the statement in the new mission that includes a commitment to Anishinaabek visibility and a land acknowledgment. I'm ready to start referring to that when we request things.

Lin: I've said this to you: if we were a land-grant institution, this conversation would be one hundred and thousand ten percent different.

Andrea: Michigan State could not handle the two of us together.

Lin: I struggle with the labor expectations that institutions have of Indigenous students. They have to go through all these hoops to put on programming and request funding. They say it's an opportunity to teach our youth how to be leaders. I've responded by saying, "See my student sitting over there? They're leaders in the community just by sitting in that space."

Andrea: Yes. Exactly.

Lin: So the institution forces them into this colonized box of what leadership is; you've got to submit an application, you've got to put this in; you've got to present to counsel; dah, dah, dah, dah, dah, day. It's just mind blowing how much pressure we put on our students and then say we're a student-centered institution. At the same time, the institution hasn't recognized that each community has different levels of struggles when it comes to showing up and participating. To dream Indigenous futures is dreaming big. We need the people in power to care. If you've got people in those top positions that just don't care because it doesn't fit their vision or it doesn't help them reach their academic and professional goals. We've talked about this before. If you're more worried about your promotion to the next position, then you've essentially become nonfunctional. You can't challenge the system and still expect to grow professionally and increase your income and your title.

Andrea: What you said is important to note especially for the audience of this collection. You said it earlier about your own path; you've chosen to not advance professionally and to stay here. I'm having similar kinds of reflections around choosing not to go into certain administrative roles. Like, because I think that in both of those scenarios, at one point you're more indebted to the institution than we are in our roles—

Lin: To our community.

Andrea: Exactly. And so and I feel like for me, even when I came here, that was the challenge, . . . to explain to people [that] I will always side with the community. I will always side with the community even when it pisses off people who will praise me, write me letters of support, or put new opportunities in my lap. And I've seen those opportunities go to other people and I've never regretted it. Ever.

Lin: Yeah. Good.

Andrea: I think that that's an important teaching to provide [for] academics here interested in decolonial work. Doing this work is not going to gain the favor of the institution or discipline. Often you're ignored or moved to the margins or tolerated. We're already complicit in the institution, and it doesn't want us to grow while we are trying to remake the institution.

Lin: It's my place to fight for my community. And you know, I shared this with my boss the other day. It's a fine line between being passionate about the work and burnout and the effects of constantly having these battles. I like this work now. It might become too frustrating, and I don't know what happens then.

Andrea: This is something I've said to multiple admin in the provost's office during the land acknowledgment workshop. I was like, I'm fine right now, but if you want to keep me, I can't keep doing this, and in the next ten years I will be done.

Lin: Yeah.

Andrea: I'll be no use to anybody. Our community believes in All Our Relations—in sustainability. My entire academic life I've witnessed academic Native women burned by the institution for doing exactly what we've done, what we're doing. Malea Powell, my mentor, says that the institution will never love you back. I'm at this point in my career where I'm not trying to get the institution, or my profession, to love me. I'm just trying to create a space where I can thrive; not just survive, but thrive, as well as students and staff.

MIIGWETCH

Andrea: I want to end by saying how grateful I am for you and how much you've taught me. I've grown in ways I couldn't ever anticipate. I always wanted a job just like this, even though GV makes me so angry, and in so many ways I'm so unhappy in my job—the thing that keeps me here and gives me joy is doing this work with you and Simone and with the counsel, and for our students and with them. So I think that's just something I wanted to end on.

Lin: Aw, I appreciate that. I want to echo the same thing since meeting you and being a part of the work at Grand Valley. I have no desire to ever be an academic. You have to put all of that work into research and advancing the discipline. You are doing it all: the research, advancing your discipline, teaching, community work. You have the added responsibility of giving a shit about the community.

NOTES

1. NAAC is a university committee within the Division of Inclusion and Equity comprising faculty, staff, and students.

2. For a period of time, the university was without an Indigenous-identified staff person to support the students. The community members fiercely advocated for the creation of a full-time position. Because of budget cuts, the initial position was half-time and made three-quarter time, which made it extremely difficult to achieve success. Additionally, we needed to persuade administrators that it was essential for someone from the community to be hired into this role due to how Indigenous families perceive institutions of higher education.

3. Michigan State University in East Lansing, Michigan, which is about an hour from GVSU.

INDEX

EDITORS

Lisa King (she/her) is an associate professor of rhetoric, writing, and linguistics in the Department of English at the University of Tennessee, Knoxville, and one of the co-chairs of the American Indian Caucus of NCTE/CCCC. Her research and teaching interests are interdisciplinary, based on cultural rhetorics and contemporary Native American and Indigenous rhetorics. More specifically, she focuses on the rhetorics of cross-cultural sites such as Indigenous museums and cultural centers, developing cross-cultural pedagogies through Indigenous rhetorics. She is the coeditor of *Survivance, Sovereignty, and Story: Teaching American Indian Rhetorics* (2015) and author of *Legible Sovereignties: Rhetoric, Representations, and Native American Museums* (2017). Her current work focuses on decolonization as part of the relationship between public Indigenous self-representation and place, including museum sites in Europe, but also at home at UTK's McClung Museum as co-curator of the Native Nations–based exhibition "Homelands: Connecting to Mounds through Native Art."

Andrea Riley Mukavetz (she/her/kwe) is the community engagement manager for Owaashtinong (Grand Rapids), the second largest city in Michigan. Prior to this role, she was an associate professor at Grand Valley State University. Her research draws from and models Indigenous paradigms, specifically from Anishinaabeg communities. She coauthored *You Better Go See Geri: An Odawa Elder's Life of Recovery and Resilience* (2021) and published more than fifteen articles and chapters related to Indigenous and cultural rhetorics. She is a member of Chippewas of the Thames.

CONTRIBUTORS

Belinda (Lin) Bardwell (Odawa) is the senior advisor on Native American Affairs and assistant director of the Office of Multicultural Affairs at Grand Valley State University. She is a former Tribal councilor at the Little Traverse Bay Bands of Odawa, where she is a Tribal citizen. Bardwell served her community for eleven years with the Native American Education Program for Grand Rapids Public Schools before beginning her advocacy at Grand Valley State University. There she continues to advocate for greater visibility for our Anishinaabe community's American history and ways of being. Her advocacy work also took her to Standing Rock during the Dakota Access Pipeline resistance in 2016 and 2017, where she brought needed supplies to the Michigan Water Protectors. Her work there resulted in an Emmy-nominated documentary titled *We the 7th*. She also produced *Ngiiwe: Shaping Narratives*, an Emmy-nominated documentary about reclaiming the relationships and traditions of her ancestors. Bardwell has a master's of public administration degree, lives in Clarksville, Michigan, and is the mother of four beautiful Odawa children.

Yavanna M. Brownlee, is an assistant professor in English at the University of Northern Colorado (UNCO), where she teaches composition, cultural studies, and Indigenous literatures. Her teaching focuses on multicultural identities and literacies, along with feminist, queer, and environmental concerns. Her publications currently include an article in *Enculturation*, "Relational Practices and Pedagogies in an Age of Climate Change," and a forthcoming chapter in *Teaching Composition in the Age of Catastrophic Climate*

Change, edited by Russell Mayo and Justin Everett. When she is not teaching, running the International Film Series at UNCO, or writing, Brownlee likes to spend time with her family and her chickens.

Christina V. Cedillo (she/they) is an associate professor of writing and rhetoric at the University of Houston-Clear Lake. Cedillo's research draws from cultural rhetorics, critical race theory, disability studies, and decolonial theory to focus on embodied rhetorics and rhetorics of embodiment at the intersections of race, gender, and disability. Their work has appeared in *College Composition & Communication*, *Rhetoric Society Quarterly*, the *Journal for the History of Rhetoric*, *Composition Forum*, and various other journals and edited collections. Cedillo's current project examines spatiotemporal tropes that affect how marginalized rhetors and their messages are perceived and received based on modernity's colonial/modern epistemics. They are also the lead editor of the *Journal of Multimodal Rhetorics*.

Deidre Anne Evans Garriott (she/her) is a professional track instructor and the Writing Center director at the University of South Carolina in Columbia. Her research draws from cultural rhetorics, material and place-based rhetorics, and social and racial justice to focus on Southern identity, in addition to writing center tutor training, community engagement, and administrative burnout. Garriott has published and contributed to two edited collections, *Space and Place in the Hunger Games: New Readings of the Novels* (coedited with Whitney Elaine Jones and Julie Elizabeth Tyler) and *Writing Centers and Racial Justice: A Guidebook for Critical Praxis* (2023) with Talisha Haltiwanger Morrison. Her work has also appeared in *ePortfolios@edu: What We Know, What We Don't Know, and Everything in-Between* and *Interpreting and Experiencing Disney: Mediating the Mouse*. She and Haltiwanger Morrison are currently drafting a writing tutor guidebook that centers tutoring from social justice orientations. Her other current projects study colonial memory and World War II memory in the US South.

Catheryn Jennings (Cherokee Nation) is an assistant professor in the Department of English, co-director of first-year writing, and affiliated faculty in environmental studies at Hamline University in St. Paul, Minnesota. She received her doctorate in rhetoric and writing at Michigan State University and received her BA and MA at Northeastern State University in Tahlequah, Oklahoma, her hometown and Tribal community. Jennings's research and teaching paths include work in first-year writing, writing across the curriculum, Indigenous rhetorics, land rhetorics, and composition pedagogy. She is a managing editor for *constellations: A Cultural Rhetorics Publishing Space.*

Malea Powell is a professor of research in the College of Arts & Letters at Michigan State University, where she is a faculty member in American Indian and Indigenous studies. She is a former editor of *College Composition and Communication*, lead organizer of the Cultural Rhetorics conference, director of the Cultural Rhetorics Consortium, founding editor of *constellations: A Cultural Rhetorics Publishing Space*, past chair of the Conference on College Composition and Communication, and editor emerita of *SAIL: Studies in American Indian Literatures*. A widely published scholar and poet, Powell's current book project, *The Medicine Path*, examines the continuum of Indigenous rhetorical production in North America, from beadwork to alphabetic writing to traditional medicine practices. In her spare time, Powell does beadwork, makes herbal medicine, reads tarot, and hangs out with other aunties, artists, poets, and healers.

Jaquetta Shade-Johnson is a citizen of the Cherokee Nation and an assistant professor in the Department of English and the Program for Writing and Rhetoric at the University of Colorado Boulder. Her research at the intersections of cultural rhetorics, Indigenous studies, digital storytelling, and environmental humanities is primarily focused on how Indigenous communities make meaning through rhetorical, embodied, and storied relationships with the land. She currently serves on the editorial board for *Peitho*, the journal of the Coalition of Feminist Scholars in the History of Rhetoric and Composition; on the executive committee for the Conference on College Composition and Communication; and as a founding member of the Collective for Cherokee Ecology and Foodways.

Cindy Tekobbe is an assistant professor of critical feminist science and technology at the University of Illinois Chicago. She is co-appointed in gender and women's studies and communication. As a feminist media scholar, her research is interdisciplinary and includes feminist, digital, environmental, and Indigenous rhetorics, media and communication studies, critical theories, and social justice. She is the author of *Indigenous Voices in Digital Spaces*, and her work appears in journals such as *Information, Communication and Society*, *Present Tense*, *First Monday*, and *Journal of Multimodal Rhetorics*. She is a 2023–2024 Public Voices Fellow of the OpEd Project and a 2024–2025 Fellow of the Institute for Research on Race and Public Policy. She serves as a co-chair of the American Indian Caucus of NCTE/CCCC and the faculty sponsor for the University of Illinois Chicago Indigenous Graduate Students Association (IGSA). She is a member of the Choctaw Nation of Oklahoma.

Luhui Whitebear is an enrolled member of the Coastal Band of the Chumash Nation with Huastec and Cochimí ancestry. She is an assistant professor in the School of Language, Culture, and Society for Indigenous studies at Oregon State University. She is also a mother, poet, and activist.

Kimberly Wieser-Weryackwe is a professor of English at the University of Oklahoma and affiliated Native studies and environmental studies faculty. Her book *Back to the Blanket: Recovered Rhetorics and Literacies in American Indian Studies* is part of the Recovering Languages and Literacies of the Americas Initiative, funded by the Andrew W. Mellon Foundation. Wieser-Weryackwe is a co-chair for the American Indian Caucus of NCTE/CCCC and a managing editor for *constellations: A Cultural Rhetorics Publishing*

Space. She has coedited multiple issues and symposia on antiracism in rhetoric and writing studies with Ersula Ore, Christina V. Cedillo, Rachel Jackson, and Ana Milena Ribero, publishing in *Present Tense, Composition Studies, College Composition and Communication, Rhetoric Review*, and *constellations*. In the spring of 2024, Wieser-Weryackwe served as Watson Visiting Distinguished Professor of Rhetoric at the University of Louisville.

BOOKS IN THE CCCC STUDIES IN WRITING & RHETORIC SERIES

Decolonial Possibilities: Indigenously Rooted Practices in Rhetoric and Writing
Edited by Lisa King and Andrea Riley Mukavetz

Transnational Assemblages: Social Justice and Crisis Communication during Disaster
Sweta Baniya

Memoria: Essays in Honor of Victor Villanueva
Edited by Asao B. Inoue, Wendy Olson, and Siskanna Naynaha

The Hands of God at Work: Islamic Gender Justice through Translingual Praxis
Amber Engelson

Queer Techné: Bodies, Rhetorics, and Desire in the History of Computing
Patricia Fancher

Living English, Moving Literacies: Women's Stories of Learning between the US and Nepal
Katie Silvester

Recollections from an Uncommon Time: 4C20 Documentarian Tales
Edited by Julie Lindquist, Bree Straayer, and Bump Halbritter

Transfer in an Urban Writing Ecology: Reimagining Community College–University Relations in Composition Studies
Christie Toth with Joanne Castillo, Nic Contreras, Kelly Corbray, Nathan Lacy, Westin Porter, Sandra Salazar-Hernandez, and Colleagues

Teachers Talking Writing: Perspectives on Places, Pedagogies, and Programs
Shane A. Wood

Materiality and Writing Studies: Aligning Labor, Scholarship, and Teaching
Holly Hassel and Cassandra Phillips

Salt of the Earth: Rhetoric, Preservation, and White Supremacy
James Chase Sanchez

Rhetorics of Overcoming: Rewriting Narratives of Disability and Accessibility in Writing Studies
Allison Harper Hitt

Writing Accomplices with Student Immigrant Rights Organizers
Glenn Hutchinson

Counterstory: The Rhetoric and Writing of Critical Race Theory
Aja Y. Martinez

Writing Programs, Veterans Studies, and the Post-9/11 University: A Field Guide
Alexis Hart and Roger Thompson

Beyond Progress in the Prison Classroom: Options and Opportunities
Anna Plemons

Rhetorics Elsewhere and Otherwise: Contested Modernities, Decolonial Visions
Edited by Romeo García and Damián Baca

Black Perspectives in Writing Program Administration: From the Margins to the Center
Edited by Staci M. Perryman-Clark and Collin Lamont Craig

Translanguaging outside the Academy: Negotiating Rhetoric and Healthcare in the Spanish Caribbean
Rachel Bloom-Pojar

Collaborative Learning as Democratic Practice: A History
Mara Holt

Reframing the Relational: A Pedagogical Ethic for Cross-Curricular Literacy Work
Sandra L. Tarabochia

Inside the Subject: A Theory of Identity for the Study of Writing
Raúl Sánchez

Genre of Power: Police Report Writers and Readers in the Justice System
Leslie Seawright

Assembling Composition
Edited by Kathleen Blake Yancey and Stephen J. McElroy

Public Pedagogy in Composition Studies
Ashley J. Holmes

From Boys to Men: Rhetorics of Emergent American Masculinity
Leigh Ann Jones

Freedom Writing: African American Civil Rights Literacy Activism, 1955–1967
Rhea Estelle Lathan

The Desire for Literacy: Writing in the Lives of Adult Learners
Lauren Rosenberg

On Multimodality: New Media in Composition Studies
Jonathan Alexander and Jacqueline Rhodes

Toward a New Rhetoric of Difference
Stephanie L. Kerschbaum

Rhetoric of Respect: Recognizing Change at a Community Writing Center
Tiffany Rousculp

After Pedagogy: The Experience of Teaching
Paul Lynch

Redesigning Composition for Multilingual Realities
Jay Jordan

Agency in the Age of Peer Production
Quentin D. Vieregge, Kyle D. Stedman, Taylor Joy Mitchell, and Joseph M. Moxley

Remixing Composition: A History of Multimodal Writing Pedagogy
Jason Palmeri

First Semester: Graduate Students, Teaching Writing, and the Challenge of Middle Ground
Jessica Restaino

Agents of Integration: Understanding Transfer as a Rhetorical Act
Rebecca S. Nowacek

Digital Griots: African American Rhetoric in a Multimedia Age
Adam J. Banks

The Managerial Unconscious in the History of Composition Studies
Donna Strickland

Everyday Genres: Writing Assignments across the Disciplines
Mary Soliday

The Community College Writer: Exceeding Expectations
Howard Tinberg and Jean-Paul Nadeau

A Taste for Language: Literacy, Class, and English Studies
James Ray Watkins

Before Shaughnessy: Basic Writing at Yale and Harvard, 1920–1960
Kelly Ritter

Writer's Block: The Cognitive Dimension
Mike Rose

Teaching/Writing in Thirdspaces: The Studio Approach
Rhonda C. Grego and Nancy S. Thompson

Rural Literacies
Kim Donehower, Charlotte Hogg, and Eileen E. Schell

Writing with Authority: Students' Roles as Writers in Cross-National Perspective
David Foster

Whistlin' and Crowin' Women of Appalachia: Literacy Practices since College
Katherine Kelleher Sohn

Sexuality and the Politics of Ethos in the Writing Classroom
Zan Meyer Gonçalves

African American Literacies Unleashed: Vernacular English and the Composition Classroom
Arnetha F. Ball and Ted Lardner

Revisionary Rhetoric, Feminist Pedagogy, and Multigenre Texts
Julie Jung

Archives of Instruction: Nineteenth-Century Rhetorics, Readers, and Composition Books in the United States
Jean Ferguson Carr, Stephen L. Carr, and Lucille M. Schultz

Response to Reform: Composition and the Professionalization of Teaching
Margaret J. Marshall

Multiliteracies for a Digital Age
Stuart A. Selber

Personally Speaking: Experience as Evidence in Academic Discourse
Candace Spigelman

Self-Development and College Writing
Nick Tingle

Minor Re/Visions: Asian American Literacy Narratives as a Rhetoric of Citizenship
Morris Young

A Communion of Friendship: Literacy, Spiritual Practice, and Women in Recovery
Beth Daniell

Embodied Literacies: Imageword and a Poetics of Teaching
Kristie S. Fleckenstein

Language Diversity in the Classroom: From Intention to Practice
Edited by Geneva Smitherman and Victor Villanueva

Rehearsing New Roles: How College Students Develop as Writers
Lee Ann Carroll

Across Property Lines: Textual Ownership in Writing Groups
Candace Spigelman

Mutuality in the Rhetoric and Composition Classroom
David L. Wallace and Helen Rothschild Ewald

The Young Composers: Composition's Beginnings in Nineteenth-Century Schools
Lucille M. Schultz

Technology and Literacy in the Twenty-First Century: The Importance of Paying Attention
Cynthia L. Selfe

Women Writing the Academy: Audience, Authority, and Transformation
Gesa E. Kirsch

Gender Influences: Reading Student Texts
Donnalee Rubin

Something Old, Something New: College Writing Teachers and Classroom Change
Wendy Bishop

Dialogue, Dialectic, and Conversation: A Social Perspective on the Function of Writing
Gregory Clark

Audience Expectations and Teacher Demands
Robert Brooke and John Hendricks

Toward a Grammar of Passages
Richard M. Coe

Rhetoric and Reality: Writing Instruction in American Colleges, 1900–1985
James A. Berlin

Writing Groups: History, Theory, and Implications
Anne Ruggles Gere

Teaching Writing as a Second Language
Alice S. Horning

Invention as a Social Act
Karen Burke LeFevre

The Variables of Composition: Process and Product in a Business Setting
Glenn J. Broadhead and Richard C. Freed

Writing Instruction in Nineteenth-Century American Colleges
James A. Berlin

Computers & Composing: How the New Technologies Are Changing Writing
Jeanne W. Halpern and Sarah Liggett

A New Perspective on Cohesion in Expository Paragraphs
Robin Bell Markels

Evaluating College Writing Programs
Stephen P. Witte and Lester Faigley

This book was typeset in Adobe Garamond and Myriad Pro by
Barbara Frazier.
Typefaces used on the cover include Garamond and News Gothic Std.
The book was printed on 50-lb. white, offset paper.